I'm no one's Obedience got me here

Committed to being Submitted

Unto the Lord

Committed to being Submitted

Unto my own husband

By; Janee' Perks @2018

Kanesha
Janaiya & Mya

Janee' Perks
9/8/18

I'm No One's Girlfriend & Obedience got me here

Copyright © 2018 Janee' Perks. All Rights Reserved.

No part of this book may be reproduced or transmitted in any form or by any means, electronical or mechanical, including photocopying, recording or by an information storage and retrieval system, without permission from the author.

All Scripture quotations, unless otherwise indicated, are taken from the Holy Bible, New International Readers Version, NIrV Copyright 1995, 1996, 1998, 2014 by Biblica, Inc. Used by permission of Zondervan. All rights reserved worldwide. www.zondervan.com The NIrV and New International Readers Version are trademarks registered in the United States Patent and Trademark Office by Biblica, Inc.

ISBN-13: 978-1987739459
ISBN-10: 1987739450

CreateSpace
Available from Amazon.com

Written by Janee' Perks
Edited by Stephanie Parrott
Foreword and Acknowledgements Edited by Alexus Applegate

Cover Design by Erica Bledsaw @ Erica Denise Entertainment
Cover Photo by Albert Jones @ Jones Photos

For information contact : Janee@noonesgirlfriend.com

I'm No One's Girlfriend & Obedience Got Me Here

Foreword By

Pastor Vincent E. james Sr.

It is with great excitement and honor that I get the opportunity to introduce to you an incredible and amazing woman of God, Janee' Perks. Janee' is one of those rare people you come across in life which leaves you wanting to be better, but most important, Janee' leaves you wanting more of Jesus. If you are around Janee' for more than thirty minutes, you soon realize that she is a woman who is open, honest, and transparent in sharing who she is and what she is about! Some might say that Janee' is a bit of an idealist in thinking that one life can really make a dent in the world, but I would say that Janee' is the ultimate realist; someone who believes that God is really who He says He is and that the true reality of this life is to follow Him wholeheartedly.

The book that you have in your hand, **I'm no one's Girlfriend & Obedience got me here,** may just be the most transparent book outside of God's Word you will read this year. The status quo and norms of the so-called "Christian" life that many are used to experiencing are in for a shock! In this book Janee' beautifully weaves her life experiences into a tapestry of life's ups and downs that will help you to understand your purpose and place in the Kingdom of God. She demonstrates how the power of God can help you overcome the power of the flesh and keep you pure to do God's work. You will be amazed at the unique style she delivers both a powerful and personal word to each reader with a sense of urgency that seeks to awaken a sleeping believer mired in the comfort of middle ground.

I'm no one's Girlfriend & Obedience got me here is the perfect title for this book because it helps you to truly understand that we belong to God and obedience allows our lives to be lived to its fullest potential. Why is **obedience** to **God** important? **Obedience** to **God** proves our love for Him (1 John 5:2-3), demonstrates our faithfulness to Him (1 John 2:3-6), glorifies Him in the world (1 Peter 2:12), and opens avenues of blessing for us (John 13:17). Janee' demonstrates her love for God and how faithfulness helped her experience the blessing of God in her life.

I am challenged to the core by the pages you're about to read! I'm excited that you are diving into this much-needed book. I really want to encourage you to face up to the strong convictions of **I'm no one's Girlfriend & Obedience got me here.** I know your heart and spirit will be stirred again for your faithfulness to God to move to another level.

Vincent E. James Sr.

Senior Pastor Elim Baptist Church

I give this book back to the Lord

Prologue-

"For your Glory" (by: Tasha Cobb)

Hello everyone! Thank you for taking time to support me in this new endeavor of becoming an author. This book is so special to me. I'm overwhelmed and undeserving to be chosen by God, to carry out such a task. I'm a thirty-three-year-old black woman of God. Single with no kids. I'm a Licensed Cosmetologist who enjoys doing hair. But after eight years of being in the field, I discovered doing hair didn't bring me joy. Being able to minister to my clients, pray with them, uplift and be uplifted, is what brought about joy. It's something about sharing God's word and my own testimony that ignites that fire. Standing on God's word that we shall overcome by the blood of the lamb and the words of our testimony *Revelation 12;11*. OBEDIENCE and being unashamed to tell my Testimony got me here! Giving all glory back to God, instilling hope in someone else that yes, you can make it, even through that. Whatever your "that" is. Most that know me consider me private. That's true to a certain extent. The truth is, I don't like small talk, I don't do that well. But I can sit and talk for hours if someone is listening, and you want to talk about real life happenings or the word of God. I'm an introvert. You will more than likely catch me by myself. My career as a stylist has taught me how to interact with people and come out of my shell. I also serve as Worship Leader at my church and most recently became the choir director for the youth choir. This has taught me to be more open and transparent with people, which in turn, makes me more relatable.

Growing up I was surrounded by a lot of successful women. Between home and church there were nothing but career driven women with big titles. But no one ever shared with me how to get there, how they made it, or how to overcome life's obstacles. I am the only girl of four. I needed a big sister. My mom did her very best! She says to this day that she didn't know what to do with a girl. She just threw me in with the boys. Though my two younger brothers are eight and fourteen years younger than me, I had only one younger female cousin in the same house, and three other male cousins. They were all like brothers. Actually, by the time my little brothers were born, I played more of a mother role than a big sister role. Growing up being the oldest girl of us two, I needed an example. Someone to have those talks that I couldn't have with my mother. Someone to tell me where not to bump my head because they had already experienced that. Not having that big sister figure for myself made me want to become that for my clients, my niece, goddaughters, and now for any woman that will listen. My passion for wanting women to be the very best is so strong. Wanting women to see themselves past their insecurities, and self-doubt. To truly know how God sees us.

I consider it an honor when the youth compliment me on what appears to be success. I've heard "Ms. Janee' you are goals" or, "you're really doing well for yourself." Glad that everyone can celebrate what God has done, but not wanting them to see just the glory. A lot has come with where I am in life, and I've had to endure much to get to this "glorious" place. Some blessings God just handed me, without me asking. There are others for which I had to give up something in order to receive them. Showing God that He is Lord over my life, and not people or things.

I've been told I'm holier than thou and I'm too saved. I try to apply my life to the word. That one confused me the most, I thought that's what I was supposed to do in this Christian walk. Hearing "you're always at church." Or the saying I can't stand "you church people." Yes, there are some folks who are just church, Sunday morning people but fortunate for me, I aim to not be one of them.

It hasn't always been this way. Before I didn't know how to be friends with women, or even be a woman's cheerleader. Quite naturally having all brothers meant I excused all "brothers." I always found a way to have the guy's back, completely dismissing the woman. When you grow up running with the guys and gain several male friends along the way, you become one of the guys in your thinking. I would hear their stories and it seemed funny at first. Then life happened and I became that woman on the other side of those stories. I found myself saying, "Wait a minute! I'm a woman too! I'm a woman first." Brother or no brother, some behavior was no longer acceptable and I didn't always have the relationship with Christ that I have now. Before, my relationship was with the church and there's definitely a difference between the two.

The dating world wasn't that kind to me. But I wasn't always so nice to me either. My struggle with loving myself caused me to tolerate any and everything. I chased the idea of being in love. Not realizing that what I was experiencing wasn't love. I have now decided to chase God and not a man. God, Jesus Christ in heaven, loved on me in a way that I never thought was possible for me. When I made God the lover of my soul my world began to change.

I have always enjoyed writing. For years that was my only way to communicate. In school I wrote letters, poetry, and short stories. In relationships I wrote letters, emails, and really long text messages to express how I felt. Writing is one of those secret things that I do and I never letting anyone read what I write or journal. But God started placing it on my heart to write a book. This was something I had never even thought of. What would I even write about? I knew whatever I wrote needed to be real, transparent, and relatable to all women. This type of transparency, having to go back in my mind and remember situations I tried to bury, has brought about many tears. More tears came when I acknowledged that. Just because I can handle my truth, doesn't mean everyone else would be able to. I became self-conscious and concerned with who would be offended and feel some type of way. I held back in the first five drafts of *I'm No One's Girlfriend,* but I kept hearing God tell me, "there's more" over and over. Knowing that surrendering brings him glory, and me healing, and freedom, I finally just let everything I had inside of me flow out through the tips of my fingers and onto my keyboard. The reality is, no matter how saved I am now, I still fall short. I have a past and it wasn't clean. I chase God now, but before, He was chasing me and I didn't always answer. Even in God knowing all of my past, he still chooses to use me. OBEDIENCE got me here, is what I refer to as my baby that was hiding. When God revealed I had two books, I thought I had two separate books. Never thinking to combine the two. Now it makes complete sense. I learned I wasn't a girlfriend while walking in OBEDIENCE. I don't have it all together by any means and I'm nowhere near perfect. Reading God's word *(specifically Deuteronomy 28)* I learned that the consequences that came with being disobedient, made for a far more difficult life and I made the smartest choice of the two: OBEDIENCE.

I use scripture as a reference for this book. It's God's word that helped me to change my way of thinking as a single woman. You will notice that I use titles of worship songs to name my chapters throughout the book. The songs listed ministered to me during this process of healing and changing and becoming who God called me to be. The Worship Leader in me often finds a song that expresses just where I am. Feel free to listen to the songs as you read through the chapters.

My goal isn't to expose anyone. Again, my ultimate goal is to encourage women to raise our standard for how we view ourselves, to teach how God views us, and to share what happens the moment we submit our lives to Christ and put him first. I believe if we knew how precious we are to the Most High and that he ultimately has our best interests at heart, if we truly knew and trusted him, that we would stop allowing anything from anyone and not be concerned with the opinions of people.

I'm No one's Girlfriend & OBEDIENCE got me here

CONTENTS

Introduction: "Intentional"	14
1. "Let Your Power Fall"	23
2. "Free"	34
3. "Your Love"	44
4. "Turning Around For Me"	59
5. "Jesus Will"	68
6. "Destiny"	84
7. "Moving Forward"	91
8. "I am What You See"	97
9. "It Was Necessary"	114
10. "I'm Getting Ready"	120
Inspiring Worship Songs	*131*
The Word Say's	*132*
Acknowledgments	*134*

Introduction

"Intentional" (by: Travis Greene)

"I'd rather this be awkward with you, than without you." The voice on the other end of the phone, said nervously to me.

Struggling to be vulnerable and express his love for me in a way that he had never done before, he continued.

"I've never been able to say this to any woman before… I need you. I need you in my life."

That conversation in May 2017, those few words, shifted the relationship between myself and the guy that I considered my male best friend, but called my brother. I'd heard him voice his attraction for other women, and he heard about pretty much every guy I ever dated, was "talking" to, or even found attractive. We were the best of friends. Everything I could talk to the girls about, I could share with him. He was one of the only male friends I had that never tried me. We called each other brother and sister because we were so close. We have experienced so much together in the last three years. Comedy shows, road trips, gospel concerts. We scheduled annual lunch dates just to check in on each other. I rode my first roller coaster with him at a camp we went to together for a week with the youth at our church. He covered me in prayer in a way I had never experienced from anyone. We taught Sunday school together. Attended weddings together. He took me to my first NBA game. We created phrases that we would say to each other, phrases that only he and I knew the meaning of. He was my ace!

It could have been the times that he came and fed me, knowing I was in the salon all day and hadn't eaten, that set him apart from other male friends. That happened often. When he learned about me not eating, he came to the salon with grocery bags full of things for me to snack on while at work so that I wasn't starving my body. It could have been the time I was a part of the prayer ministry at the church and felt under attack, and he came and prayed over me. We would come to church two hours before service started and pray over the church. Laying prostrate on the floors praying, walking the choir stand, praying over the musician pit. Inviting God to come in and bless the service that would soon take place. One Sunday, I laid in a spot of the church and felt like someone was standing over top of me kicking me down. I kept getting up to look around to make sure no one was there, and it wasn't. What I felt was so strong, I became distracted in trying to pray. My Pastors sermon that day taught on women being raped, and how never dealing with it causes us to hold back in being who we were called to be. The spot I laid in that morning was close to where the guy normally sat who had raped me years ago. I always struggled with trying to figure out if I did something to lead him on or not. Blaming myself for possibly making the wrong move, that made him think I wanted it.

Or maybe my "NO" wasn't stern enough. I only told one person, my female best friend, and I let it go. I tried to bury it, thinking it was my fault, and unsure if that is what truly happened. It wasn't until about 2 years after it had taken place that my god sister came to visit me from college. She was telling me and my female best friend about a protest that was taking place on campus. Some white girl was accusing this black guy of raping her, and the black community on campus wasn't having it. I know now it was only the Holy Spirit that made me ask her what his name was. If you could have seen the look on my face, when she said the name: It was the same guy who raped me.

My female best friend and I were both screaming. I remember I kept yelling, "I told you! I told you! She's not lying, he did it to me too."

That was the day I thought I was finally free. I was no longer tripping. What I thought happened, happened. The day he walked into the church where I was serving and showed up every Sunday for at least two to three years, is when I realized I wasn't over it. I would sit from the choir stand, wondering "who else has he violated? How does he treat the woman he was currently with?" I would wonder what he was thinking, seeing me week after week. When my male best friend learned of this, he came the next Sunday to prayer and prayed over me. He stood with his hands on my back, as I was seated in the church pew and covered me. He stood in place, blocking anything that was going to try to come up against me spiritually.

The shift happened for me in our friendship when he called me asking questions about his kids. I knew him well enough to know that his kids meant the world to him. He didn't trust just anyone with them. He asked me questions that required me to have to be completely honest with him, questions that he could have asked anyone. He would call me and say, "I know you will tell me the truth." I knew at that point he trusted me. Knowing that he had that type of trust in me let me know I wasn't just another female friend that he had. We had developed a true friendship here.

He dated one of my female friends. Yep, you heard correctly. She is more of a sister than a friend. Girl code to the natural eye is broken, right? Crazy thing is that two years prior to this conversation that he and I was having, she told me that I should consider him as more than just a friend. "You have everything him and those girls need," were her exact words.

Originally, I thought she was tripping, and I cried. I couldn't receive what she was saying. Fast forward to this thing manifesting. I'm honored and blessed to have such a mature friend. She didn't deny the great man that he was and she said that she recognized the friendship and chemistry we shared. Thank you, Renee, I love you girl.

He and I played a game several days prior that led us to this conversation.

"Describe the characteristics of the person you think would be best for me" ...

Shortly after we began describing each other's ideal mate, we realized, we had described ourselves for each other. We were everything for one another that we wanted in a spouse.

"Have you ever considered us?" I nervously asked. Nervous and afraid of the rejection, because I knew my best friend and his "type." He likes darker women, I'm pretty light skinned. He's a butt man, I'm top heavy. Most of the women he was interested in were skinny. I wear double digits! Nothing skinny about me. Total opposite of what he was into.

"I never thought about it until now." He responded

We had heard it before. People always questioned if we were just friends, or immediately would assume when they saw us with each other that we were a couple. It was the forehead kiss that he always planted on me affectionately that had people convinced that we were more than what we claimed to be. That was just who he was. I never thought anything of it. The time we went to camp with the youth, the ladies in my cabin told me I should start looking at him as more than a friend. They watched how, all week while at camp he watched after me and made sure I was comfortable, being this was my first time going. Still, I thought nothing of it because I knew him to be a caring person to everyone. I wasn't thinking there could possibly be an us. Often times we were offended when people would make us each other's "you might as well." We *hated* that. Don't "might as well" us! "You might as well" sounded like we should just be settling. Without hesitation, we always corrected people with "oh no, that's my brother," or "that's my sister."

Days after the awkward conversation we were given an assignment. We had been asked about a month or two prior to be part of our church's first ever coed prayer brunch. There would be men and women partnered to pray over a specific topic for ten minutes each. The Minister in charge of the brunch had explained that she wanted my best friend and I to do a topic, and closer to the event she would give everyone their topic that they were assigned to pray on. Being partnered with my best friend came as no surprise. We thought nothing of it. We had done other things in the church together outside of working with the youth. We were featured in a video advertisement for a prom that our church hosted each year. So, this was no big deal. The surprise came when I was given the envelope that had our topic listed as relationships/marriages as our prayer target for the coed brunch. It made absolutely no sense to me that they asked the two-single people in the church to pray for relationships and marriages. Confident that this was a part of God's plan, my best friend told me to go ask the minister in charge why she picked this subject for us. He felt it would ease my mind if I talked to her. Speaking with her I expressed how this wasn't making sense to me. She agreed. She didn't know why, but God kept telling her that he wanted my best friend and myself to do it. She went on to tell me that she even went to write a married couples name down that was participating in the brunch as well to do the topic, and God said no. My best friend and I were who he wanted to do it. She told me she just surrendered and did what God was telling her, all that was left was for me to surrender.

With this new discovery of us possibly being an item, things began to change. We grew even closer to each other. Often having moments of, "is this real?" Mind blown at God and how all this time, everything we wanted was right under our noses. You hear that said all the time, but it felt unreal to be experiencing it for myself, especially when I wasn't looking for it.

Typically, each party in this scenario would be over the top excited. You found true love when you weren't looking. Your best friend is the love of your life. He wants you, you want him, but that wasn't the case. God had intentionally removed the scales from our eyes and allowed us to see each other differently in His timing, in a way that only He could have done so. But something kept holding me back. There was something in me that couldn't receive him for myself. I kept wrestling with the fact that he dated my friend, even though she said she was ok. I wasn't. God had spoken to me a year before this telling me I had to leave her behind, because she was going to hold me up. I had no clue what God was referring to in that moment. Now I believe he knew this would be a road block for me. I also had never dated a guy with kids before and a man with kids never made it on my checklist of who I wanted my man to be. He didn't just have kids, he had custody of his kids and that was extremely different. I knew some weekend fathers, but not many single, full-time fathers.

My unsettledness didn't stop everyone else from going on about it. Family and friends grew excited when they saw me post about my best friend on Facebook, using the hashtag #bestfriendisbae, or my Instagram post with a picture of us captioned, "Dating my best friend." For me being as private as I was, this said a lot. Ring the alarm, after 5 years of being single, Janee' has a man. People were ecstatic! Comments, text messages, and screenshots were all being shared. Those who didn't already know him couldn't wait to meet him. Those who knew him were elated for us. To the eyes of many this was amazing. To some, a few eyebrows were raised knowing he dated my friend. So many questions people wanted to know. Are you still celibate? Do you cook for him? Do you do his daughters' hair? When I would answer these questions, "Yes, I'm still celibate, no, I don't cook any more than I did before this and no, I don't do his daughter's hair. I'll teach them to do their own hair." Each time I answered these same questions with these same answers. I was made to feel like I wasn't doing something right. Did me being in love require me to add these things to my to-do list? Are these things a must in order to have a relationship? Being a girlfriend was becoming less and less attractive. Why was so much expected to only be a girlfriend?

    The more I sat back and thought about my previous relationships, I realized that I did all these things plus some. I cooked, cleaned, synced my schedule with theirs. A couple of exes lived with me *and* drove my car. One didn't even have a car at all. I wasn't a girlfriend. I was acting as a wife, and some cases a mother to these grown men. I didn't want any of that with this. I wanted to do something different, and he did too.

"I'm sorry, I can't be with you. I'm no one's girlfriend."

Chapter 1.

"Let Your Power Fall" (by: James Fortune & FIYA)

February 15, 2016, I decided it was time for some new furniture. I was only supposed to be looking. However, the impulsive me ended up swiping my debit card all in the name of the President's Day sale that ended that day. The price for a sofa and accent chair was one that I couldn't resist.

As I walked the aisles of the furniture store, browsing and weighing my options, I walked up on a couple having a disagreement. He liked something and she wasn't feeling it, at all. I began to think to myself how lucky I was to be single. I had the freedom to pick what it was that *I* wanted. I took my thoughts even further, recognizing that I had made the decision on my own that morning, to make a large purchase. Realizing that at some point in these two, unidentified people's lives, they had to come to some type of agreement that this is what they wanted to do with their money.

I didn't have that worry, that burden. I was free to make decisions for myself. The only person I answered to was God, and He had already given me the okay. This encounter made me think back on so much that I had done. Purchases made, places I've gone, future trips locked in with the girls. It made me realize that, if I were married, I couldn't, well, shouldn't do these things without talking them over and getting my spouse's approval. This ah-ha moment was happening as I was getting closer to entering my fourth year of being single. It took me that long to appreciate my singleness.

I had three "boyfriends" in my 33 years of living. Well, four if you count this short-lived relationship you just read about in the introduction. Everyone else was just something to do. Something happened on the inside of me after the third break up. I was tired of going through the cycle of relationships. I was depressed when things didn't work out with the third boyfriend. I found myself questioning God and why things completely ended. I was used to my ex and I breaking up and making up. Even though I ended things, I wasn't expecting him to stay gone. When it started looking like God wasn't working on my behalf, I made my own will for my life and started working for Him. Even after being told to be still. I wanted to get my ex's attention. I wanted to show him I loved him and that I was the one. Being told to be still didn't make sense to me. Being still wasn't going to help me get the attention of who I believed to be my husband. Meanwhile I was dying, doing cartwheels, backbends, and somersaults trying to make things work. I was just like the Israelites needing a bronze snake, needing protection from dying from the poisonous snake bites because God wasn't taking the pain away. I had to learn to look up.

"They traveled from Mount Hor along the route to the Red Sea, to go around Edom. But the people grew impatient on the way; they spoke against

God and against Moses, and said, "Why have you brought us up out of Egypt to die in the wilderness? There is no bread! There is no water! And we detest this miserable food!" Then the Lord sent venomous snakes among them; they bit the people and many Israelites died. The people came to Moses and said, "We sinned we spoke against the Lord and you. Pray that the Lord will take the snakes away from us." So Moses prayed for the people. The Lord said to Moses, "Make a snake and put it up on a pole; anyone who is bitten can look at it and live." So Moses made a bronze snake and put it up on a pole. Then when anyone was bitten by a snake and looked at the bronze snake, they lived." Numbers 21:4-9

Looking up asking God to reveal himself to me, I had been in church all my life but had no relationship with Christ. Baptized at the age of thirteen, not because I knew anything about God dying for my sins. I did that because I loved singing in the youth choir. I used to get up every first Sunday during communion, walk out of the choir stand and leave out of service because I wasn't taking it. Apparently, this was a distraction. So, the Pastor created a new rule. In order to be a part of the choir, you had to be baptized. Well sign me up! I wasn't going to miss out on being in the youth choir because I hadn't been dipped. I was extremely shy in my younger years and I still am to this day. The boldness that people see now comes from nobody but the Lord, when I'm operating in what he's called me to do. Which is why most that have never seen me while ministering don't even know I sing because I'm so shy. Not even the men that have lived with me.

At thirteen I went to the Pastor and asked him if I could get baptized in private. I didn't want the entire church to see me. He agreed to doing so, as long as I came to the front of the church and confessed Jesus Christ as my Lord and Savior. Agreed! To my surprise, when the day of my baptism came, my Pastor at the time announced there would be a baptism going on after church, if anyone wanted to stay. "She's a little shy," he said over the mic. I had about 10 to 15 people there. It was a little more than I would have liked but I made it through.

Singing songs became normal growing up because I loved music. Showing up week after week out of routine. Attending every gospel concert put on. But still, I had no personal relationship with God. There was always a tug on me to want to know God more. Sitting in bible study every week hearing about the one who died for me always interested me, but before now, it was never enough to make me give up the lifestyle I was living. Wanting to try something other than what apparently wasn't working for me after this third break up, I began to read God's word and find out who God is. I went all the way to the beginning in Genesis. It was one thing to hear someone else tell me what scripture said. When I began to read the bible for myself however, I was able to see where God had been moving in my life all along. My dipping date wasn't as life changing as the date I decided to submit my life to Christ. No disrespect to the idea of being baptized. I know God honors baptism (*Matthew 28:19*). I actually considered getting baptized again, knowing I did it for all the wrong reason initially. However, there has been nothing more rewarding, memorable, or life transforming than the encounters I had with God. To experience him has kept me with him.

    The first year of being single (2012-2013), I journaled about a study I attended for singles. Examining every fine detail of what I needed to be to become a wife. We broke the story of Songs of Solomon down. My male best friend was just another guy at my church to me during this time frame, we didn't talk much. It came as a surprise when he walked up to me one Sunday after church and told me that God told him to tell me to get ready because he was going to be sending me somebody. It startled me so badly I remember dropping my lipstick that I was holding in my hand. During this time my male best friend was newly single as well and a few folks around the church kept trying to play match maker. I wasn't interested and I knew he had an interest in someone else. Normally I would be leery of someone telling me "God said." I've seen that be abused by people in the church, wanting you to conform to their own agenda. This was different. God knew I would be suspect of what news he was sending me, so God did something right before this to make me aware that he would be using my male best friend as a messenger. At bible study, days before he came to deliver the message, I was singing on the praise team. My female best friend and I were sitting next to each other in the choir stand, and my male best friend was participating in a skit. As I watched the skit, I saw a bright light around him. I swung and hit my female best friend so fast, asking if she had seen that but she was clueless as to what I was talking about. I asked someone else, "did you see that?" Nothing! I didn't have a clue why I saw that glow around him and no one else did. When he approached me with the message from God, I took it as a symbol from God letting me know he was going to be a messenger.

In this first year of singleness working out and healthy eating became a lifestyle change for me. I transformed my physical body. Though this was a good change, however, it didn't last because I hadn't made the change for me. I did it thinking it would get the attention of the one I wanted to be with. I had always felt like he was ashamed of me because of my weight. I believed that if he saw me transformed he would want to get back together. It only worked temporarily and now, I know size has nothing to do with love. I began separating myself from who I no longer wanted to be. I quit the club life and going out every weekend. I did away with my Facebook account for four years. I wanted to no longer compare my life to those on social media. I wanted to see what God said about me. I began working on getting my finances in order. I broke up my debit card and gave myself a $50 weekly budget to go toward anything outside of bills. I still purchased things that I wanted. It just took a little longer saving my weekly allowances until I had enough to get myself what I wanted. This helped me to become disciplined in the area of finances. I went to Kay Jewelers and purchased myself a ring as a sign of my commitment that I was going to dedicate this time with God and live a life of celibacy. (Since the first year of my purchasing a ring, I've actually upgraded myself twice.) I became a student of God's word. My prayer life increased and I began talking to God about any and everything. I activated my faith and began to step out and trust God.

I began walking in faith in different areas of my life. I needed a new car, but I knew my credit was horrible at the time. Reading God's word and listening to sermons had me convinced that if I believed and walked in faith, God could work with the impossible. He did just that. After praying about getting a new car, something I wanted, not just what they would give me, I walked boldly into the car lot and test drove the car I was interested in, (a Dodge Charger), trusting God to restore what I had lost. I told the salesman the price I was willing to pay monthly for it and he came back almost an hour later with payment amounts almost one hundred dollars less! I went into the restroom at the car lot jumping, praying, and giving thanks. God had showed up on my behalf! At the time I was working two jobs to make ends meet and a student at school. When school was ending, God told me to quit my part time job at UPS and do hair full time. My time there was up. "Two jobs are for two people. You don't need that second job, you need to trust God." My Pastor said that twice in two different sermons after I heard from God. I knew God was speaking to me. He showed me a scripture in *Ecclesiastes* that confirmed it was time to let UPS go. When I was OBEDIENT my clientele became more than enough to sustain me, even more clients kept coming in.

"There is a time for everything, and a season for every activity under the heavens"- Ecclesiastes 3:1

God had sent me a close friend that year. He was a new neighbor in the apartments I lived in. He treated me in a way that I had never experienced being treated by a man before. It became hard to not be attracted to him. I thought God was sending me my man. He was so kind and treated me with so much respect. He made me question what it was that I had been putting up with from other guys. I did something I had never done in the past: I asked God what this relationship was supposed to be. He gave clear instructions using the story from *2 Kings:4;* this man wasn't someone I was to date, but he would help get me out of the depressed state I was in. He did just that. Even after being told that, I still had a hope that this could turn into something. Wanting to be loved so bad, I sent myself through unnecessary heartbreak because God had already told me what it was.

Outside of the idea of my neighbor not being the one, I was experiencing God's overflow in other areas of my life. Believing God for anything. My faith was so high. I trusted God with my life. If God was able to do all this, plus so many other blessings, bringing me my husband was going to be nothing!

The closer it was getting to entering my second year of singleness, I thought I'd activate my faith even more. I began proclaiming marriage over my life for that year. I went to bridals shows because I wanted God to see me walking in faith, trusting for this thing. I was turning thirty that year and the only thing that I felt was missing from my life was a husband. God and I were about to work together to make this happen though, no worries! I heard God tell me my wedding date was going to be July 19, 2014, the day of my 30th birthday. It fell on a Saturday that year, so how perfect was this going to be! I wrote out a guest list, went to find dresses, the whole nine yards. The only thing missing was a groom! Closer to the date however, God showed me I wasn't going to marry a man. I was marrying myself. I needed to fall in love with me. The only problem was, I had no clue what that looked like. That night, on an emotional high of my birthday, I was willing to risk my new walk, and throw my commitment to God out the window. I planned to give myself to my neighbor. He was there at the party I had thrown for my big 3-0 and had asked me to call him when I got in. After my party was over, my cousins, some friends, and myself went to a club to continue the celebration. When we finally came out of the club, both my cousin's, and her boyfriend's cars had gotten broken into. My phone went dead and, for whatever reason, I didn't have a car charger and no one else did either. I was so frustrated. This was messing up my night and Shively Police took their sweet, precious time getting there. I couldn't even send my neighbor a text to let him know that this operation was still in full effect. After the two hours that it took the police to finally come up the street, it was so late that I just went straight in the house and went to bed. I know now that this was God's way of blocking what I was about to do. Sorry Cousins!

By the third year of singleness I felt like I was ready to go out there and see what life had to offer! I chose to be more open and attempt to date. This is when I really found out it was easy to practice celibacy as long as you were by yourself. It was a whole other ball game when you had flesh in front of you. Flesh that made you laugh and catered to you. I would often discount anyone that talked about sex, feeling like he's not the one. The one for me wouldn't even mention it, think of it. He would willingly stop having sex for me. Quickly, I had to learn that lesson as well. It would be the man that loved God enough to wait for Him, not me. In this third year, I learned more and more for myself. Just because I wasn't sexually active, that desire didn't just disappear. If I was struggling with trying to refrain from sharing myself with a man that I was interested in, how much more does a man with no commitment to God struggle? I was saying no, but still wearing the same revealing clothes that excited their flesh. I had to learn to take my attire in consideration. I needed to make sure my appearance wasn't sending the wrong message.

God woke me up out of my sleep in the middle of the night, the night my new furniture was delivered. I hadn't had time to figure out what I was going to do with the furniture I currently had because remember, I wasn't planning on buying so soon. But that sale! I had two living room suits and two dining room table and chair sets sitting in my apartment. I fell asleep watching a movie on the couch that night and now I was up looking at all this... stuff. God said, "get rid of the old, so you can make room for the new. The new is already yours and in your possession, but it can't take its rightful place until you get rid of the old." In complete amazement, I got to work clearing out the old the next day. This was bigger than just the furniture. I went through my entire house getting rid of anything that I didn't need or use anymore. God wasn't just talking physical, he was talking spiritual as well.

Chapter 2

"Free" (by: Kierra Sheard)

Getting rid of things wasn't an easy process. Some thoughts and important documents I held on to because I never wanted to forget how far I had come. I never wanted to repeat the same cycles, so holding on helped me to keep a wall up that wouldn't allow me to get hurt again. Some things such as jewelry and clothes I held on to with the hope of being able to use them again, possibly fit into again. The memories of people I held on to, hoping to one day relive the joyous moments. Some memories helped me identify red flags for the not so delightful moments. My strong grip on the things I was holding on to caused me to self-sabotage. Not allowing room for anything or anyone new to enter my life. These next few chapters may have been the most difficult yet. Quite naturally, I'm a cry baby. I'm sensitive. It doesn't take much before I'm red in the face. There was a season in my life however, that I grew numb. Experiencing so much pain just from life happening. Some that I allowed, and some that I couldn't control.

Once I begin to walk this single life out, I got more and more comfortable with myself and in God. I reached a place that I had to go to. I needed to seek becoming whole. I was believing I needed someone else to complete me when truly, no one else can complete who God intended me to be, not the unique version of me. Another person can add to who you are but they can't complete you.

This was a time to unpack the luggage that I had been carrying. A time to find out who I was and discover the things I liked and didn't like. I was guilty of taking on the hobbies of my boyfriends in the past. Their favorite team became my favorite team. I couldn't tell you the history of the team or a player, but would go all in. And occasionally, I would find myself sitting down watching the game. Now, I'm not saying there's anything wrong with allowing someone to introduce you to new things. Because of boyfriends, I learned I like basketball over football and one boyfriend introduced me to a world of music that I had never experienced. I'm talking about not having my own identity, so much so that I became who *they* were. Everything I did was based on what they liked. As soon as that relationship was over however, I dropped that sport, hobby, or habit, and picked up whatever the next guy in line liked. Now, here I was during my single years, left asking myself, "Who am *I*? What do *I* like?

I had to ask myself those, what seemed to be two very simple questions, but because I never took the time to get to know me, I would often have to fish for answers. We're quite naturally habitual people, and life is a routine to us. We often find ourselves in cycles. This cycle showed up in my relationships as well, I met a guy, I fell in love, invested what felt like my all into a relationship that, more than likely, I knew I shouldn't have been in in the first place. Eventually, we'd go through our ups and downs. Most of the time, I'd be feeling like I invested more in the relationship than the other person involved, and before you know it, I'm left trying to figure out what happened and what went wrong with me. This was my time to HEAL.

Until I made up my mind that I was tired of bad relationship after bad relationship, I continued to fall into this routine. The routine of not allowing my heart to fully love, not allowing myself to receive love, the same fears, arguments, and the same type of men. It became a continuous cycle until I took the time to heal. It wasn't just my heart that I had to heal from heartbreak after heartbreak. I had to heal my soul from all the soul ties I could become entangled from being with someone who wasn't my husband. I was only told not to get pregnant. No one told me the power of sex. I had to heal because sex can truly control you and cause you to get out of character, making you think that you're in love when love is far from what's really going on.

Soul Ties- Souls being knit together to become one.

"Do you not know that he who unites himself with a prostitute is one with her in body? For it is said, "The two will become one flesh." –
1Corinthians 6:16

I'm not talking about that "out of sight out of mind" healing. The, "you haven't seen him, so you're over him" type of healing. Or the, "to get over one man, you get with the next man" healing. Actually, that is a lie from the pit of hell. You get with another man if you want to, it's still the same damaged you, with your same damaging characteristics that will eventually come out. Now there is more luggage to unpack.

I'm talking about time to myself, me and the Lord and getting to the root of the issue. I'm talking about finding out what triggered me, and why, dating myself, learning to love my own company, treating myself to a movie and dinner. I'm talking weekend getaways out of town by myself and attending events alone that I wanted to experience without allowing the fact that I had no one going with to stop me from going. I'm talking about doing whatever I like to do, and doing things to find out if I liked it or not. I'm talking about getting rid of the old! I'm talking about being free.

During this private time with the Lord, I learned a lot of my issues came from the fact that my biological father wasn't there. You hear growing up how important the daddy/daughter relationship is. I can remember growing up feeling like that didn't apply to me. The hurt, bitter part of me never wanted to give him credit for how I was. Even the negative parts of me. I didn't want to acknowledge that his absence meant something. I felt like it would be giving him power over my life. Not knowing that not addressing the issue of him not being there and the effect it had on me, was me giving him power. I decided to take my power back.

When I began to realize my biological father played such a major role in how I acted toward men, and what I allowed from men, it was a true eye opener. My feelings of abandonment in my childhood years came from him and, carried over into relationships. So much so, that when I was with someone, I needed to be reassured constantly that this is where they wanted to be.

My biological father's mother lived next door to me growing up. There was a season when he lived there as well, yet he still wasn't involved in my life. When he moved out of my grandmother's house, I can only remember one time going to his place. That one visit of him leaving me with my brothers and sister, never him interacting with me. I saw him, knew he was my dad, but there was nothing that connected us. I constantly need to feel connected in my relationships. It's never enough to just be there. My struggle with broken promises came from my biological father as well. He would always tell me that he was going to do something for me or get me something, and it never happened. My mom was always left to pick up those pieces. I need assurance for that too in relationships. Don't tell me you're going to do something, and not do it. I would bloop. This forced me to over compensate in that area. If I committed to something or gave you my word that I was going to do something, I didn't care how much sleep I gained or lost, I did what I needed to do to honor that. I knew what that let down felt like.

I was thirty-one when I first heard my biological father tell me I was beautiful! Do you know how many men I looked to for that confirmation? I can remember when he said it. I immediately began thanking God that He had been a Father in his place. The Lord had already showed me way before that moment how beautiful I was. Hearing these words for the first time from my biological father, made me appreciate God even more.

It was hard for people to understand that yes, my stepfather was there, but because I knew who my daddy was, I wanted that relationship. It was something about wanting that love from him and only him. I remember as a child, one year for Christmas I wanted a Vtech computer. My biological father promised and promised I would get it for Christmas and guess what? I never got it on Christmas. I want to say however, that he eventually got it, or he end up giving my mother the money to go get it. Either way, the disappointment was there when I woke up Christmas morning to nothing from him. When my stepfather learned about this, (he was just the boyfriend at the time) the next Christmas came around. He purchased me a desktop computer because that's what I said I wanted. I was excited, but unappreciative because I desired my biological to do these things.

I had my biological father's phone number in my phone for a couple of years as an adult before I actually used it. He would deliver a message to call him thru my brother when they would run into each other. I always wondered why he never asked for my number. I mean, I was the child. Why was it my responsibility to reach out to him? I never felt the need to use his number until the day the third boyfriend and I broke up. I called him, angry, asking why he didn't do what he was supposed to do, telling him that he was the reason I didn't know how to love. After that conversation we arranged a visit. He blamed my mom for his absence in my life. This caused my anger to grow because I had been over eighteen for at least ten years at this point, and still no effort on his part. I never called him back until a few years later, when I was mature enough to have the conversation without playing the blame game or being angry for what he didn't do. I asked to do lunch with him. I let him know that I didn't want to know what happened. I just wanted to get to know him because I was trying to learn who I was. After lunch and a few more outings that I initiated, accepted who he was and the role he wouldn't play in my life. I came to terms with the fact that he was my father, he even loved me, but had no clue how too. When I allowed that to settle in, I was finally able to move forward.

    It took years before I could truly appreciate my stepfather, or to understand that a man like my stepfather was what I should desire. I always knew he was a good man, but not knowing any better, twisted thinking had me convinced my stepfather was soft. I still don't know why good girls like bad boys. I used to get so angry feeling like he let my mother do and have whatever she wanted. Especially as a child watching them. I would get so mad feeling like he always catered to her. Thinking, "he does whatever she says." Why did catering to your spouse look so bad to me? Never seeing it before him is the only thing I can think of. I watched him bring his paycheck home every week and just hand it over to her. Because of my foolish thinking, this didn't make him a man in my eyes. When in all actuality, he was the example of how I should be treated and how God has commanded every man to treat his wife. The more I studied the bible and seen how God adores the church "the bride". I knew my stepfather was the best example of a man I had. Now that I'm in a different head space in my life, our relationship has grown so much. We have breakfast dates and catch up on life, just him and I. I'm still amazed at his love for my mother after twenty- five years, and his constant desire to want to please her. I know she can be a handful!!

"Husbands, love your wives, just as Christ loved the church and gave himself up to her"- Ephesians 5:25

I had to deal with the little girl on the inside of me that still wanted to be loved, never felt protected, and wanted to be a daddy's girl that wanted him to want her. I had to deal with her because she is who kept showing up in relationships unconsciously. She still may show up from time to time, but now I can identify her because I have understanding of what triggers certain emotions.

When I was a girlfriend, I searched for men like my biological father. Visible to me, but not active in my life. I remained a secret to my third boyfriend for years. Even after he lived with me, and I built a relationship with his family. I became a member of a new church, and to my surprise, the majority of his family attended. We naturally started building a relationship with one another. I would come home from church asking him to let them know about us because I didn't want them to think I was being fake. Smiling in their face, knowing good and well I was secretly going home to their, son, brother, cousin. I heard my Pastor profess several times, "you'll be known for the works of your hands, and not the man that you're with." I was unaware of what that meant until I started my cosmetology career, which began shortly after I started attending the new church. I announced my new endeavor at choir rehearsal and his family, who was now my church family, became my clients. He refused to tell them we were in a relationship and when they found out, I was still denied. Until I dealt with the little girl inside of me that still craved her father's love, I still wanted this boyfriend back and I wanted him to be my husband. I was begging him to see my worth and to consider giving us another try. He never acknowledged we were anything. We never went in public together and half the time, wouldn't speak when he saw me out. Friends and family thought I was lying about his existence. This relationship had me constantly questioning my worth. There was this one time I came home, I assumed he had company. I walked into my house to find every picture that was hanging on the wall of me, taken down. This was the day I felt he was the most ashamed of who I was. I always felt like he had a reason to be, because of my father's absence. I was sold on the idea that if my own father didn't claim me, why would any other man? I went back and forth with this boyfriend for a long time, always the guy that, in between break ups, that I ran back to. I struggled with letting go of the idea of he and I being together. Texts, emails, phone calls, and visits after the break up were enough to keep me holding on and hopeful. Now I understand why. It wasn't him that I desperately wanted. I was searching for my father. Once I dealt with the absence of my father, it became easier to let my ex - boyfriend go.

"A father to the fatherless, a defender of widows"- Psalm 68:5

"For the Lord your God is a merciful God; he will not abandon or destroy you or forget the covenant with your ancestors, which he confirmed to them by OATH." - Deuteronomy 4:31

"For he chose us in him before the creation of the holy and blameless in his sight. In love, he predestined us for adoption to sonship through Jesus Christ in accordance with his pleasure and will." - Ephesians 1:4-5

Chapter 3

"Your Love" (by: William Murphy)

Before running back and being in a relationship with the one that kept me a secret, I was with a guy who kept our relationship very public. The little girl in me that never felt appreciated, loved, or beautiful was made to feel all these things this time around. He was with me and let the world know he was with me .... and this one, and that one, and that one. When I was his girlfriend, I accepted a lot of things I never deserved because guilt ate at me.

"Therefore, there is no condemnation for those who are in Christ Jesus" Romans 8;1

If I'm not condemned in Christ, who is the world to condemn me? I have no place to condemn myself. The Lord searched my heart and fully examined me, He showed me how I walked and operated out of guilt. I over extended myself in certain areas of my life because of guilt.

When I was eighteen I had my very first "real" relationship. I can honestly say I was a horrible girlfriend. I would always do things to my first boyfriend and his car. His car was his prized possession. In order to really get under his skin, I always went for the car. Doing things like throwing things on it, or spilling things purposely in it. I drove off in it one day after an argument. He almost had a heart attack. I even went as far as keying the car in the parking lot of his job one day. If he could have killed me, he would have. He loved that car. When arguments would get heavy I'd start fighting on him, and one time, I pulled out a knife. I did all of this knowing he would never hit me. I had a half way decent guy, considering how young we were. Thinking back on it, he actually reminded me a lot of my step father, but again at that age, I couldn't appreciate a man like that. I couldn't understand him always wanting to hold hands and be affectionate in public. I had just really started experiencing sex and getting a lot more freedom at home. My first boyfriend was a student at a school two hours away from me. No, it's not far, but to have others giving me attention that he couldn't offer up, I did a lot of sneaking around. I was creeping with the secretive ex-boyfriend whom I gave my virginity to right after high school and sneaking with another guy that wouldn't tell a soul he had anything to do with me. This guy and I, we both clubbed a lot. We would walk right past each other in the clubs as if we didn't know each other. As soon as the club was over, I was letting him in my house, into my bed.

    I would always come out and tell on myself when I cheated. He would be hurt but he always took me back. He catered to me, made himself available to me. He went above and beyond to make sure I was always well taken care of. He had moments of other women wanting to creep in. Once (that I know of), fed up with my actions he allowed one to slip thru. For the most part he checked women that tried to make a move on him. He would respectfully let them know he was with someone. He talked to me about marriage and building a future. A man with a plan for us. I was too young to appreciate him.

Four years later when that relationship was over and it clicked the kind of man that I had, he was done with me. I was devastated. How did I let this happen? Why did I treat him like that? Regret set in years later when I started experiencing turmoil in my next relationship. I had met a new guy that was taking his place. I can say now, I knew he was no good for me, but like most of us that awaken love before it's time, lust feels like love.

I got with this new guy and tried to be the best girlfriend I could be. I felt so bad about how I treated the last guy that I dealt with things I had never experienced before. I was experiencing cheating, domestic violence, and other things I never thought I would have allowed. I can remember feeling like I deserved everything that happened to me. Believing this was what I was reaping because of what I had sowed in my previous relationship. I allowed guilt to tell me lies that caused me to stay in a relationship that meant me no good. Lies that made me sit back and accept abuse and believe that no one would ever want me and that I wasn't worthy of receiving love. This isn't acceptable, even if you're married. No type of abuse should be tolerated.

I believe I was at my lowest in and after this relationship. The things that I dealt with from this boyfriend took me the longest to overcome. I'm just now finding out after over ten years of being in the relationship that I suffered from PTSD. (Post Traumatic Stress Disorder). I had to get to a place of being unashamed that I was a victim of domestic violence in order for that healing to happen. I was always known to have a strong personality and back bone. It was hard to wrap my mind around the idea that I sat back and let that happen to me. I mean, I grew up fighting with boys, but this was different. I never wanted to fight the one I expected to love me.

Don't get it twisted, the relationship didn't start off that way. Nah, dude appeared to be in love with me for the first year. I was spoiled rotten and I got what I wanted when I wanted. That eventually came with a price. He was proud to have me on his arm, and that felt good. We had our typical couple issues but not enough to break us up. That is until I was cheated on early in the relationship. I left and should have stayed gone. When I allowed him back, he came even stronger. If someone thought I was spoiled the first time around, it increased even more this second run. Him spoiling me with material things, made me overlook some behavioral characteristics. Some of the drama didn't bother me at first. I didn't even see it. He had me and I had his nose wide open, one would say. We made plans to be together, we named the children we planned on one day having together. "He loves your dirty drawers," a coworker would always tease me and say, and I was in love with him too.

 Looking back now I acknowledge the role I played in this as well. To fight a dude was nothing to me. Being the only girl of 4, I grew up fighting my brothers. Even though my two youngest have such a huge age gap between us, that never stopped them from picking up something to fight me with. I hung with my oldest brother, male cousins, and their friends. Our grandfather instilled in us that if one fights we all fight. My brother stayed into it with somebody. I never had to fight for him, but never feared standing up for him. If it went there, I wouldn't have backed down. When it got to the point in the relationship where my boyfriend and I would have arguments, if it went there physically, same rules applied- no backing down. This time around, I was with someone who would hit me back. We fought everywhere; in churches, before and after rehearsals, at home. No place was exempt. And we fought in front of everyone. We would be back together before the night was over. Ike and Tina someone called us, but I wasn't getting Tina'd so, I didn't see a problem with it. It had become so normal that I didn't see how toxic this relationship was.

 Things began to turn when suddenly the girl that he first cheated on me with started reappearing. This time I decided to get even instead of crying over it. I thought I would show him I had some savage in me as well. Not only did I cheat, I cheated with someone I knew he didn't like. Someone he considered an enemy. I wanted him to hurt the way I was hurting. This is what I now believe drove him crazy. It's true when they say men can't handle women doing to them, what they do to us. It's also true that hurt people, hurt people.

I told him that I cheated when we got over the hump, but I only told him bits and pieces. A shift happened. When he learned the full truth, my life became a living hell. Looking back almost ten years later, he lost respect for me. Instead of leaving me, he stayed and made me pay for the pain he was experiencing. I started getting treated different, being disrespected, abused, and treated like I was his possession. Other men didn't feel comfortable holding a conversation with me or greeting me with a hug if he was around. He became extremely jealous. Even more women started rolling in. I started finding all kinds of things: text messages, video recordings, and cigarette butts lying around from the women he kept company with. One married woman left a business card to the girl that braided her hair in his bed. Most of the women would lie to me and say they weren't messing around, that they were just friends. My women's intuition would say otherwise, and I should have listened to her, the inner me, that gut feeling. Him being at my house most nights (he lived with me for the majority of the relationship), and me having a key to his apartment that he eventually got, led me to believe it was me he really wanted. I was there when he wasn't at my place. Which made me want to believe he didn't have time to do all the sneaking around.

I was young, naïve, immature, and super petty back then. Here for all the action, I wanted it. A mug here and a push there. There were even times he would break my belongings and pour things on me. It wasn't until I quit fighting back that things got worse. When the fighting got worse later in the relationship, other people got involved. I called my cousin to come over a couple of times. He and my brother would show up never knowing the story, and I honestly never wanted them to hurt him. I just wanted their presence to intimidate him. They would walk right in the church and check dude for me. I never told my cousins or brother all that was happening to me. I knew my family and never wanted to be the reason any of them were behind bars for trying to defend me. Instead of leaving I kept staying because, 1) I was being told everything I wanted to hear and it sounded better than the reality I was facing. 2) By now I was separated from the world and made to believe he was the only one that loved me. He no longer liked any of my friends. I allowed him to separate me from them, believing if I left, I wouldn't have anyone. Friends/people had grown so disgusted with the drama that came with us. They wanted nothing to do with us. 3) I was blaming myself for why things were happening and wanted to stay to fix it. 4) My pride wasn't going to let him go. I felt like I had something to prove to everyone that said we couldn't work and I wasn't about to let the next female feel like she won. 5) I eventually became scared of him and believed he would kill me. This was a side of him I hadn't seen, so I didn't know what he was capable of.

      Breaking up with him wasn't an option until I learned how he was trapping my windows so that they appeared shut and locked but really weren't. I had my apartment broken into several times whenever I would try to terminate the relationship. I was a heavy sleeper so one night I woke up tied up, with him standing over me, telling me how he would take my life. Another time, he ripped my panties off and raped me, trying to get me pregnant in hopes I wouldn't be able to leave. Once, I woke up being choked around three in the morning, after he hid in my walk-in closet all night. This traumatized me the most. For years I would have to check every room in my house to make sure no one was in there. To this day, I've been told that if someone wakes me up, I'm jumpy or I look frightened. I had been kicked, slapped, nearly choked to death, burnt with black & mild's, dragged down steps and spit on. He was constantly popping up at places, because he knew my routine. His look alone would intimidate me. Afraid for my life, I went and purchased a folding hunting knife to carry. My work shift had changed to a later time. I walked at least three blocks from my job to the parking garage. I wanted to be able to protect myself if he walked up on me while leaving work. One night in my own home, I thought I was going to have to use it. He ran up on me with a kitchen knife, so I went to get the knife I purchased, and started coming after him with it. When he noticed my attempt to protect myself, this made him angry. He tried everything in his power to get this knife out of my hand. Knocked to the ground, I laid flat in my walk in closet floor with the tightest grip on my knife. Knowing, if I let it go, it was a possibility it would get used on me. My arm was bruised from the punches it took, from his attempt to make me let go of the knife, hearing him tell me in a deep voice that I never heard from him before, to let it go. Sleeping with a tainted man, I became just as poisoned. I can remember times of me screaming and yelling, begging for him to get it together, wanting to work through whatever twisted sickness this was. Playing on the girls' phones, who were "just friends", becoming mad at them. He would be driving one of the girl's car around. Once I caught him in her car and I even followed them. I should have been done but something in me wouldn't let me leave. I would show up to his apartment acting a fool when I would catch them together and throw sticks at the windows. Once I caught him and busted through his apartment door swinging, with the car still running, driver's side door opened, parked in the alley. I was ready to fight whoever. We would end up separated after these moments but be back together by night. Continuously breaking up and making up. I started experiencing suicidal thoughts, unsure why this was happening. Why was I experiencing so much hell from the man that claimed to love me? All I wanted was for things to go back to the way they were in the beginning.

That didn't happen. Here I was, catching black eyes, and still having to argue with these females that thought they wanted what I had. "They have no clue what's happening," I would say when no one was looking. By this time, people were starting to see, but not too many would say anything. The one's that did speak up, I was too hard headed to listen. The last black eye was the worst. I almost lost my eye sight in my left eye, he hit me so hard. Arguing outside of an apartment complex, we turned to walk away in opposite directions from each other. Then, for some reason, we both turned back to face each other at the same time. As I was turning, I didn't realize he was swinging his fist. My face made direct contact with his fist. That punch was so severe that I fell asleep for a brief second. I assume someone saw this happen, because the police came. Sitting there in disbelief, I hid in my car behind my dark tint, dazed, still not wanting to get him in trouble. I couldn't even drive myself home, he had to come drive me. The next morning my eye was completely shut swollen black, purple, and blue. I got dressed for work but the more I stared at myself in the car mirror, I knew I couldn't go to work. I could picture the stares and hear the whispers that would take place if I went in looking like this. Instead, I had him drive me to Walgreens to get some medicine for the pain. I went home and put a piece of raw meat on my eye. Later that day I found out, not only were my items purchased but money was also taken from my debit card for him and the woman he was cheating on me with to go to lunch, sending my account into the negative. I knew then he could care less about what just happened.

I had to take off from work for at least a week before make-up was enough to cover the bruise. Here I was, calling into work, risking losing my job. I ended up going to the hospital. I made up a story saying that someone threw a candle and it hit me in the eye. Typing that out, I now know how silly that sounds. My eye was so bad, the white area of my eye (sclera) was completely blood shot red. I had to go to see an ophthalmologist twice a week for about a month. I was eventually able to get FMLA for work because I was having to miss so regularly. Doctors had to find the blood vessel that had burst to stop the bleeding. That required getting dye shot into a vein in my arm so they could find which vessel in my eye was busted. Once they found the vessel, I had to get a needle stuck into my eye because I was seeing black dots in the center of things and nothing appeared straight. Letters and sentences on the computer at work looked like they were floating. My retina was scarred from the punch, and I was told that there was no way to fix the retina. I was told I wouldn't be able to see a straight line ever because of this. That one punch has affected my life. To this day, I worry about losing my vision in my left eye. Certain days it will ache really bad, especially when it rains. Sinus problems or headaches are the worst. Most of the pressure is felt in the left eye. I often have times in my profession when trimming hair or shaping someone up, I close my left eye to make sure I have an accurate cut. Years later I see where God was still with me, concerned about my vision when I went to take my state board test to receive my cosmetology license. The hair cutting portion of it I sectioned so well and took my precious time. The lady grading me and watching me told me she watched me cut it to perfection so she didn't need to check it. Thank you, God, for always being with me.

    I found out how real demons were in this relationship. One night, I found myself backed into a corner fighting and somehow, I ended up on the floor under the dining room table begging and screaming, wanting the fighting to stop, but it kept going. Then suddenly, my mouth started moving and words that I wouldn't be able to repeat if I tried, came out. I had no control over anything that was coming out of my mouth. I couldn't make it stop. Whatever I was saying caused him to calm down. It went from him fighting me, to him comforting me, asking me what was wrong and what was I saying. He was completely calmed down from the words that were coming out of my mouth. I know that God spoke through me to that demonic spirit, using His own language/tongue that has power.

    The fighting got so bad that police and later down the road, an EPO were involved. False hope of us working through this and coming out of this slowly faded away. The first time he was arrested we were riding up the street, arguing in the car. I pulled over and he got out. I attempted to leave, and he jumped on the hood of my car. Standing on top of my car in this parking lot, screaming and yelling at me, he kicked my windshield in. When he did this, he didn't notice the police officer right up the street that just so happened to see everything. Since our driver's licenses didn't have the same address on them. He was under arrest. If we would have lived together at that time, I would have had a choice whether or not I wanted to press charges. But because we didn't live together he was arrested for destruction of property. I spent money I didn't have on jail calls. And they were right, a man in jail will tell you anything. Once he got out things still remained the same.

Somewhere in all this chaos, one of his "just friends" got pregnant. When I finally learned of this, he apologized, told me it was a mistake, and begged to stay. THIS WAS ANOTHER WAY OUT, but I was too young and dumb to take it. Instead I tried to get pregnant by him but it never happened, and now I thank God that it didn't. I believed every lie, including the lie that he still wanted us to work. I held on to who he was at the beginning, praying that that person would show up again. The one who loved on me and catered to me. Trying to ride whatever phase this was, out, my riding almost caused me to die. Some nights I felt like I was literally fighting for my life.

I remember us laying in the bed and the phone call he received the morning it was time for the delivery of his child. At first, I was being told he didn't want to go that morning, he wasn't ready to be a father. That quickly turned into, "I'm going to be with my family by night." I became outraged feeling like this girl and her child ruined my life. The words I condemned myself for for years saying when arguing with him, "I hope you and your child die," came out of my mouth. I was sick with it. Being in that position with no self-control, allowing rage to control me. Hurting once again by him, I wanted him to hurt and all I had were my words. You truly don't know what you will do or say, in certain situations, until it's you. I felt like everything that I worked hard for with this man was thrown out the window. I needed somewhere to place my anger. I laid around the house for days, laying in the middle of the floor, depressed. Feeling like life couldn't go on without him. I had made him my god.

    After the early birth of the baby I attempted to stay, and I was miserable. I blamed everyone but me for being in this mess. Guilt ate at me when the child did actually pass away. Life only got worse because he too, blamed me for his child's death. Eventually, there was another child conceived. By then however, I had finally grown tired. Tired of being lied to, and mistreated, tired of being sick. Afraid of catching an STD. Clearly no protection was being used on their end, and none on ours. It was time to go. I had a dream one night, of someone on a stretcher being taken out of my apartment. There was a blanket over the face, I don't know if it was me or him. I just knew at that point, I needed to make my exit. Or this wasn't going to end well.

"Wash away all my iniquity and cleanse me from my sin" Psalm 51;2

Chapter 4

"Turning around for me" (by: VaShawn Mitchell)

After each break up with him I fell for the Glory! This was a set up. I would see him operating in his gift, talent, call as a musician, and it looked good on him. As a matter of fact, this is when he appeared the most attractive to me. It was something about seeing him in that element that always brought about peace. That's what had kept me constantly going back. I would get sucked back in gig after gig. I later learned it was no longer him that I was attracted to, it was the glory of God that fell on him when he was in that element. It wasn't him I longed for, I confused the attraction of God's glory with love for this man. God can use anyone or anything he pleases to bring himself glory. The real question I had to ask myself was, "who was this man when God wasn't using him?" I needed to pay attention to *that* person, because that was the real, authentic him. Who was he when no one was looking? One thing I've learned is that fruit doesn't lie. The fruit someone is producing, will tell you just who that person is.

"By their fruit you will recognize them. Do people pick grapes from thornbushes, or figs from thistles? Likewise, every good tree

bears good fruit, but a bad tree bears bad fruit. A good tree cannot bear bad fruit, and a bad tree cannot bear good fruit." Matthew 7:16-18

That time in my life was an emotional roller coaster, but God took me and all my stuff and unpacked it, piece by piece, one bag at a time. The troubles the Apostle Paul says that will come with marriage don't even look like this. And I was accepting it from a boyfriend. God dealt and revealed so much about me to me. I had repented, and He had forgiven me. He didn't allow me to play victim either. He corrected me with the things I initiated, and areas where I was out of order. He dealt with me and my tongue and showed me how to use my words to uplift. God has taught me how to say truth in love, and how to handle conflict without wanting to put my hands on someone. He taught me also to forgive myself and others.

We are blessed to serve such a forgiving God. Not just to me, but all of us involved in these painful relationships. I knew I was healed when I could pray for my ex-boyfriend and the women I was cheated on with. Crazy as all this was. Over the years with time, prayer and healing, my ex and I are able to converse. We apologized to each other and are cordial with each other. There are limits to what I allow from him. But I no longer tolerating being misbehaved. God loves and forgives us all, who am I not to.

"The tongue has the power of life and death, and those who love it will eat of it's fruit." - Proverbs 18:21.

"For if you forgive other people when they sin against you, your heavenly Father will also forgive you. But if you do not forgive others their sins, your Father will not forgive your sins."- Matthew 6:14-15

He said to her, "daughter, your faith has healed you. Go in peace and be freed from your suffering." - Mark5: 34

Here I am years later, just now understanding why I kept taking him back, hit after hit. A side from the obvious, low self-esteem. My oldest brother was the example of a man that I watched closely growing up. There was a time I felt honored to be surrounded by guys, feeling like they kept me ahead of the game. Feeling like it was impossible to get played because I had seen it all, mostly from my big brother. I watched him play women left and right. I watched his drama filled relationships explode one minute and come back together the next. This is why I thought my first boyfriend was boring. There was no action. It was my oldest brother and I that would fight each the most growing up. I was a tomboy for a very long time during high school. Growing up we would fight over things like me wearing his clothes, or chores. The most frequent fight was about the phone. We grew up during a time when cell phones weren't as popular as today. Most people used a land line. We constantly stayed on it. We were given a time limit, but of course that never worked. We would fight like cats and dogs, fist fight, then come back like nothing ever happened. These childhood fights with my brother trained me to grow up and sweep those punches under the rug from my boyfriend. My brother would talk crazy to me, and I was trained to accept it because he was my brother. I'm just now taking my life back from him.

    For majority of my life, I've excused my brother's behavior, simply because I was taught that family sticks together. Sticking together caused me to take on his responsibilities and overlook how he mistreated women, even though he is quick to say what someone better not do to me. I've had to remind him that all women are someone's sister, aunt, or daughter. I was an enabler to my brother. When my brother didn't do, I did. Overcompensating for his oldest child, due to his repeat stays in and out of jail, not wanting her to go without because he didn't have it, or not wanting her to lose the connection with our side of the family. I practically helped raise his child and I didn't ask for any kudo's. When I made him look like a great parent, things were fine. Anytime I went against what he wanted however, I was often reminded by him, that that was his child. When it was special holidays like

Mother's Day, I would overdo for our mother, because I knew my brother would come up short.

Recently I took my niece in to live with me. She was being a typical teenage child and feeling herself, thinking she's grown. I created in my home, what I intended to be a huge walk- in closet and made it a second bedroom for her. I did it because one, I love my niece. Secondly, I got a phone call from the school she was enrolled in saying my brother was making me the Power of Attorney for her medical and school, and I needed to sign and return the papers. Needless to say I was confused. This wasn't even discussed, but I went along with it because again, my niece and brother needed me. My niece did so good for only so long with me before she was back to acting out. In her acting out she ran away and stayed gone for about a week. She called after the week and said, "I'll be there tomorrow." No, "hello", "Hey Aunt Nee." Nothing! At a loss for words as to what to say, I said, "what? who is this?" Knowing who she was, just amazed that she was calling as if everything was ok. We hung up, and I called back and asked, "what are you coming to get?" She answered all chipper that she was coming to stay. I began to really analyze her response. Why did she think this was okay? Why did she think she could leave when she wanted, cause confusion, and return like nothing ever happened? Her daddy. My brother. She had watched him for so long mishandle me and so many other women and was able to return like it meant nothing. In all my good deeds for my brother, he still managed to talk to me with total disrespect, and attempt to say the most hurtful things to get to me, and I was always expected to take him back, simply because we shared the same last name. During the time that my niece was gone. I prayed and asked God what I was supposed to do. God had sent a preached word *Exodus 9:16:* Even with having the best intentions, things don't always go as plan. God said to me, just like he said to the Israelites about Egypt, "I'm trying to bless you, but you won't let go of the people who aren't any good for you." Completely disturbed by the word my Pastor preached that I knew was for me, I went home and sit trying to process it all. Within hours, I received a phone call from a police officer that my brother and niece were arguing and I should come. By the time I returned home, I knew in order for the hell to stop, I had to be OBEDIENT and let them go. I'm no longer allowing my brother to mishandle me. I've made up in my own mind that no one gets to mistreat me and handle me anyway they please. I'm finally in a place where I know my worth, and I demand respect.

By the time I decided to let the toxic relationship go with my ex, I lost my full -time job in corporate America. Losing my only source of income and denied unemployment for months caused me to be behind on rent. I received an eviction notice and had my car repo'd. All that time invested in a man and a job, only to end up with nothing. This was the beginning of me getting to know who God was. Life seemed so upside down. God had me in a position where I had no choice but to answer the call He had on my life that I ran from for years, that of becoming a cosmetologist. I had been running for years, because it just wasn't what I wanted to do with my life. In my earlier years I wanted to go to school to either be an accountant or a journalist. I wanted to go to college, but my counselor from high school let me know my GPA wasn't getting me into anyone's university. Lord knows I barely made it out of there (high school). So, I never even attempted to apply for college. Having already completed the Cosmetology program right after high school, it seemed like my only option. I always knew it was what I should've been doing. I would tell myself that before I turned twenty-five I would go take my test to become a licensed cosmetologist. Instead, I got caught up in the life I was creating in corporate America because I didn't think I could achieve success in doing hair. God has proven his will for my life is far greater than anything I could have imagined.

    Here I was just turning twenty-five, and well past my five years that State Board allowed before your cosmetology hours expired. I had to write an appeal letter to Kentucky State Board of Hairdressers and Cosmetology, stating that I wanted to try to get my hours back as an attempt to not have to go through the Cosmetology all over again for the full 1800 hours. The letter needed to explain why I wanted to get the hours back and why I hadn't already taken the test. I prayed about what words to put in the letter, and God gave me the exact words to say. I submitted the letter, but I didn't hear back from the committee because they had taken the summer off. I started school in August anyway. I wasn't sure if I would get all the hours back, half the hours, or what they were going to do. All I knew was I had to be OBEDIENT and answer this thing that God kept drawing me to. The money that I had left I used to enroll into school, which is how the repo and falling behind on rent happened. I had a past due balance from the first time that I was enrolled in school. In order to get back in, I had to pay that. Months went by before the state board finally sent a response to the letter. They informed me that I only needed to do a refresher course of 300 hours. I was extremely grateful. I went to school the next day after receiving the letter in the mail, and when my teacher finally got a chance to check my hours, she yelled, "clock out!" I had already met my hours. I showed up, trusted God, and He made a way. Nov 3, 2009. I remember the date because it's my deceased Granny and her twin brother's birthday. It reminded me they was still with me! By this time, I had finally won the appeal case with unemployment against my old employer, which meant unemployment would be sending me back pay from June. Things were finally beginning to look up. While waiting on the unemployment case to get approved, I did hair out of my one-bedroom apartment to make ends meet. God had a plan all along.

"For my thoughts are not your thoughts, neither are my ways your ways," declares the Lord. "As the heavens are higher than the

earth, so are my ways higher than your ways and my thoughts than your thoughts." Isaiah 55:8-9

"For I know the plans I have for you," declares the Lord, "plans to prosper you and not to harm you, plans to give you hope and a future." – Jeremiah 29:11

Chapter 5

"Jesus Will" (by: Anita Wilson)

Going through this extreme healing and cleansing, I was believing I was now ready for the real thing. Marriage! After all, I had been cleansed, right? Frustrated still, not understanding why marriage still hadn't happen for me yet. I mean, I'm a great catch, others knew I was a great catch. Why hadn't "the one" seen it yet? A thirty-one -year old, beautiful woman of God, no kids, lived on my own, great career with a heart ready for love. I had been serving God as worship leader at my church for about a year by now. I had been granted the opportunity to go "Demonstrate" a worship leaders conference in Georgia, and to be surrounded by professional gospel artist and other worship leaders around the world with a passion and fire for God. This is the place where God tested my faith. The conference was held Thursday-Saturday which were my busiest days of the week at work. Being self-employed, I was afraid to take off work because there is no vacation time. I worked Monday, Tuesday and Wednesday before I left and took as many clients as possible to make myself feel secure financially that week. Headed to Georgia, God spoke and told me that I didn't go after the things that I desired because I was afraid of being broke again. Me losing my job and losing my car after that relationship had me playing it safe, and not reaching for my heart's desires. I became ok with just having enough, not wanting to over extend myself. Constantly saving, building a security blanket. I never wanted to end up in that situation again, not being able to take care of myself in case something happened. This revelation amazed me, I called my friend and shared with her what God shared with me, and made a wage with myself that I would treat myself to the Chevy Camaro that I wanted if I lost twenty pounds.

    While at "Demonstrate" I received so much valuable information about what it looked like to serve God and God's people at this capacity. This conference is the place I learned to sow a seed into my Pastor, *Philippians 4:14-19*. I learned the importance and duty of being a worship leader. How being worship leader was more than singing songs but knowing God's word and being in tune with the Holy Spirit. I attended a class on walking in my gift as psalmist. I heard several ministers and musicians refer to me as a psalmist, but never was clear on what it meant. I always thought I was just remixing songs, doing my own thing. I found out what it meant to sing the song of the Lord that was spirit led. I was granted the opportunity to attend the live recording for the "Demonstrate" album. Spirit filled experiences all weekend long! While there, I had all the money on me that I made doing hair that week stuffed down in my purse. I forgot to stop and make a deposit at the bank before I left Louisville. And because of horror stories that I heard about housekeeping at hotels going through your belongings, I carried the money on me all weekend. The Holy Spirit was so high in the service, and it was now offering time. As I went to get my offering out, I heard "give everything in your purse." I thought it was God but wasn't sure if my emotions were just so high that this was me talking. I gave a pretty nice offering that day, and all weekend to make sure I was covered in the giving area. I struggled often at events like this, thinking all they wanted was money. I'm a firm believer of paying my tithes. As of matter of fact, I pay double my tithes in faith, believing God to make that amount one day. My Pastor always says, you can't beat God's giving. I know it to be true, I've experienced the open windows of Heaven, *Malachi 3:10,* but struggled with gospel "programs" and their money lines. I prayed about it and told God to let me know if it was Him that I was hearing. It was the very last day of the conference, and God had moved in that place. I had a worship experience that I never had before. Everyone freely crying out to God. I went alone, so I had no distractions. Just me and God. It was prophesied over the house that God wanted to bless someone on June 1st, as soon as you get back home. The leader of the conference collected the last offering and I gave again. It was when he said, "don't worry if you aren't one to give $50, $100, or $500, as long as you were OBEDIENT to what the voice of God told you to give." That was my confirmation. I knew then God had spoken. I dug in my purse and found every dollar that I had. To this day I can't tell you the amount but know God has blessed me beyond whatever it was.

I returned home Saturday ready to give God my best and serving God's people with my best. That Monday June 1, 2015 I woke up and felt God telling me to go. Go get my Camaro. I drove to the car lot and told myself if the numbers aren't right you can always leave. I negotiated what I was willing to pay, they met that amount. Still afraid and trying to find a way out I used the excuse that my car insurance might go up. I had to consider all my options. The salesman was trying to convince me that it wouldn't. With much boldness he said, "call them". I called my insurance company for the quote and was told "Ms. Perks it will actually be cheaper than what you are paying for your current vehicle." It was a new car and had safety features like OnStar included with the car, which brought the price down. I left the car lot that day with my first ever brand-new car. It only had 17 miles on it. God told me to go. Now I thank God that I did it in his timing. I still haven't lost those twenty pounds though.

I wanted to do with this new blessing what I had done with all the others and God wouldn't allow it. I had tint put on every car I ever had. This one was to be no different. Each time I went to get the service done on my car, something would happen. Once the business was closing for the day. Another was over booked, and one wanted to over-charge me, because it was a new car. The tint job kept getting held up. When leaving to go to camp that summer, my step father told me he was going to get my windows done as a birthday gift to me. While at camp on the day I knew the service was scheduled, I hadn't heard from him. I know my step-father, he would have sent a picture to at least show me the work that had been done. I called to make sure everything went ok. He told me that he wasn't able to get them done, that they guy at the company that tints the windows was out. His arm was broken and he wouldn't be in for another week or so. I knew instantly that there was a reason this tint job wasn't happening. I asked the Lord what he was wanting me to get out of this. Soon the Lord revealed that I was no longer going to be able to hide behind things or people. I was entering a season that he would be calling me to the forefront. God showed me in *Hebrews 5:12,* that I was no longer on milk. It was time for me to step out. This happened especially in ministry. My pastor switched the way bible study would be ran at our church. He would do a mini service on Wednesdays that included a praise team and band and he would preach. For a year straight, I opened up Wednesday night bible study service, myself and a two-piece band. I was the only one on the praise team at the time, whose schedule would allow them to commit to doing so weekly. This is where I grew as a worship leader.

    I thought ok, instead of tint, maybe I'll purchase rims for the car. I went online and found some that I thought would look good on my car. Something that spiced it up just a notch, but still had a feminine look to it. When the rims came in I went to the business that I ordered from to have them put on. I was excited, thinking my car was about to have a new look. The mechanic came out and advised me that they had taken the original tires off but unfortunately, the rims I ordered wouldn't fit. There wasn't a rim in stock that fit the car I purchased. With the car being so new, they didn't have any in stock for that model. I knew I could have taken my business elsewhere, but I also knew there was a reason this wasn't happening for me as well. "Okay Lord, what this time?" I questioned. God showed me that the same way I wanted to change the look of my vehicle, was the same way I operated in relationships. Changing the look of the men I was with so that they begin to look like what I wanted them to look like, dressing them up to appear to look a certain way. I discovered later that this exact vehicle was placed on a vision board I had made. Just the way that it was fresh off the car lot. No extra bells and whistles. I've since been OBEDIENT and left the car just the way that it is.

    Through every blessing, I continued reading and studying God's word with my now close friends, who were new at the time. I had gotten close to some ladies from my church, Other believers that help sharpen and correct me when I allowed my flesh to show up. True prayer warriors that were interceding on my behalf. I started growing closer to these women and out of my comfort zone. Since the public and private break ups, I didn't allow people in my home, fearing I wouldn't have control of what went on in my household. Week after week I overcame that fear and begin hosting ladies nights in my apartment every Sunday with these women of God. Providing a place for these mothers and wives to come and let their hair down. My apartment went from being a place of chaos and confusion, to a place of peace. A place where many came to find rest. I opened up my home for the one who is like a sister now, to come live with me for a while. We didn't know each other that well when she came to stay. Sharing my space with someone that I barely knew and another female at that, was new for me. By the time she got her own place, God had developed a friendship between us, and we knew each other very well. We laughed and cried repeatedly with each other, shared many secrets, got on each other's very last nerve and overcame broken areas of our past together.

No longer feeling bound by anything, free to tell my story and live on, I felt like marriage had to be next. I would sit in prayer, asking the question, "Lord why hasn't marriage happened for me yet?" The Lord led me to 1 Corinthians 7. This is what helped change my way of the thinking.

1 Corinthians 7 New International Version (NIV)

Concerning Married Life

7 ¹ Now for the matters you wrote about: "It is good for a man not to have sexual relations with a woman." ² But since sexual immorality is occurring, each man should have sexual relations with his own wife, and each woman with her own husband. ³ The husband should fulfill his marital duty to his wife, and likewise the wife to her husband. ⁴ The wife does not have authority over her own body but yields it to her husband. In the same way, the husband does not have authority over his own body but yields it to his wife. ⁵ Do not deprive each other except perhaps by mutual consent and for a time, so that you may devote yourselves to prayer. Then come together again so that Satan will not tempt you because of your lack of self-control. ⁶ I say this as a concession, not as a command. ⁷ I wish that all of you were as I am. But each of you has your own gift from God; one has this gift, another has that.

⁸ Now to the unmarried[a] and the widows I say: It is good for them to stay unmarried, as I do. ⁹ But if they cannot control themselves, they should marry, for it is better to marry than to burn with passion.

¹⁰ To the married I give this command (not I, but the Lord): A wife must not separate from her husband. ¹¹ But if she does, she must remain unmarried or else be reconciled to her husband. And a husband must not divorce his wife.

¹² To the rest I say this (I, not the Lord): If any brother has a wife who is not a believer and she is willing to live with him, he must not divorce

her. [13] And if a woman has a husband who is not a believer and he is willing to live with her, she must not divorce him. [14] For the unbelieving husband has been sanctified through his wife, and the unbelieving wife has been sanctified through her believing husband. Otherwise your children would be unclean, but as it is, they are holy.

[15] But if the unbeliever leaves, let it be so. The brother or the sister is not bound in such circumstances; God has called us to live in peace. [16] How do you know, wife, whether you will save your husband? Or, how do you know, husband, whether you will save your wife?

Concerning Change of Status

[17] Nevertheless, each person should live as a believer in whatever situation the Lord has assigned to them, just as God has called them. This is the rule I lay down in all the churches. [18] Was a man already circumcised when he was called? He should not become uncircumcised. Was a man uncircumcised when he was called? He should not be circumcised. [19] Circumcision is nothing and uncircumcision is nothing. Keeping God's commands is what counts. [20] Each person should remain in the situation they were in when God called them.

[21] Were you a slave when you were called? Don't let it trouble you— although if you can gain your freedom, do so. [22] For the one who was a

slave when called to faith in the Lord is the Lord's freed person; similarly, the one who was free when called is Christ's slave. 23 You were bought at a price; do not become slaves of human beings. 24 Brothers and sisters, each person, as responsible to God, should remain in the situation they were in when God called them.

Concerning the Unmarried

25 Now about virgins: I have no command from the Lord, but I give a judgment as one who by the Lord's mercy is trustworthy. 26 Because of the present crisis, I think that it is good for a man to remain as he is. 27 Are you pledged to a woman? Do not seek to be released. Are you free from such a commitment? Do not look for a wife. 28 But if you do marry, you have not sinned; and if a virgin marries, she has not sinned. But those who marry will face many troubles in this life, and I want to spare you this.

29 What I mean, brothers and sisters, is that the time is short. From now on those who have wives should live as if they do not; 30 those who mourn, as if they did not; those who are happy, as if they were not; those who buy something, as if it were not theirs to keep; 31 those who use the things of the world, as if not engrossed in them. For this world in its present form is passing away.

³² I would like you to be free from concern. An unmarried man is concerned about the Lord's affairs—how he can please the Lord. ³³ But a married man is concerned about the affairs of this world—how he can please his wife— ³⁴ and his interests are divided. An unmarried woman or virgin is concerned about the Lord's affairs: Her aim is to be devoted to the Lord in both body and spirit. But a married woman is concerned about the affairs of this world—how she can please her husband. ³⁵ I am saying this for your own good, not to restrict you, but that you may live in a right way in undivided devotion to the Lord.

³⁶ If anyone is worried that he might not be acting honorably toward the virgin he is engaged to, and if his passions are too strong[b] and he feels he ought to marry, he should do as he wants. He is not sinning. They should get married. ³⁷ But the man who has settled the matter in his own mind, who is under no compulsion but has control over his own will, and who has made up his mind not to marry the virgin—this man also does the right thing. ³⁸ So then, he who marries the virgin does right, but he who does not marry her does better.[c]

A woman is bound to her husband as long as he lives. But if her husband dies, she is free to marry anyone she wishes, but he must belong to the Lord. ⁴⁰ In my judgment, she is happier if she stays as she is—and I think that I too have the Spirit of God."

1Corithians 7 has become my go to scripture when I need that reminder, that I'm right where I am supposed to be. I find myself when trials and tribulations come saying, "I'm glad I don't have kids" or "what would I do with a husband?" The two things I have prayed to God about and allowed the rest of the world to tell me that something was wrong with me because I didn't have either. Let's just say Granny wasn't lying when she said, "God knows what you need, and when you need it." There is no way with the life I live, constantly on the go, a workaholic, that I could handle well, all of what I was praying for. I'm sure I could manage it but some area in my life would have slacked. More than likely it would have been my home. It's one thing to worry about me, a whole other to take on a spouse and children, and to do it before I'm ready. Thank You Lord again, for those unanswered prayers. The scripture that God gave me tells me that my only concerns should be those of the Lord's, considering I'm unmarried *1Corinthians 7:32*. The knowledge and understanding gained behind this scripture is what I'm standing on regarding the relationship between my best friend and myself, which also help to bring about the title of this book.

Reading, studying, and gaining understanding of these scriptures in 1Corithians 7, Seeing what God and the Apostle Paul said about the single life, helped me to become content with the state that I am in. The crazy thing was that in this particular chapter of my bible, several verses

I had already highlighted. The verses that were highlighted were all about what it said about being a wife. I was so concerned with being a wife, and studied it, that I never learned what the word said about where I was, single. Looking so far ahead that I never stopped and looked around.

Single classes I attended all taught me to prepare to be. Never was I told how to live in this state I was in. Never knew scripture said it was better to stay in this state.

v40 *"in my judgement, she is happier if she stays as she is- and I think that I too have the Spirit of God."*

The bible teaches us in 1 Corinthians 7 *Verse 8 and 9* that it is better for the unmarried to stay unmarried, unless they weren't able to control themselves. *"Now to the unmarried and the widows I say: it is good for them to stay unmarried as I do. But if they cannot control themselves, they should marry, for it is better to marry than burn in passion."*

Lord knows how hard this life was because I had already broken the purity covenant, giving up my virginity in my teenage years. All through high school I wanted to wait to have sex until marriage and it sounded good. Once I got to experience life without a leash after I graduated high school, that went out the window. Even through this difficulty of trying to die to the desire of my flesh and refrain from being sexually active, as much as a struggle it is, I have yet to meet any man since I've been practicing celibacy that was irresistible. My mind has wandered, and flesh has gotten happy, but I haven't got to the place of "I have to have you".

As I studied this word more and more, it really just brought to life how much God doesn't honor boyfriend and girlfriends. He called us to be single or married. Boyfriend and Girlfriends are truly a man-made union. *1 Corinthians 7:1-4* talks about since sex is occurring, it should be wife, with your own husband. Husband with your own wife. God isn't against sex. He just wants, and only approves of it with our own spouse. Sex is a gift from God for married people. He is so okay with it, that in *verse 5,* He tells us to only withhold from laying with each other (husband & wife) for prayer, a time for Him. But he goes on to say don't withhold too long, because I want to prevent you from being with someone other than your own husband/wife, because temptation was there.

THIS! JESUS! It changed everything! Talk about being transformed in your mind. If God doesn't approve of this boyfriend/girlfriend union, why do we feel like we must date for years before we "take it to the next level?" Why was it deemed necessary to test drive before marriage, allowing myself to go through these mock trial periods as a girlfriend with boyfriends to see If I qualified to be their wife. The Lord teaches us how to be a friend *John 15:13-15* and how to live two ways: married or single. What appears to even look like a boyfriend/girlfriend experience in the bible is with the Samaritan woman in *John4,* when Jesus called her truth out. The man she was with wasn't her husband. This made me stop and think of how many men I spent time with that weren't my husband. How many men have I submitted to that weren't my husband? How many men had I let unwrap my gift, that was only attended for my husband?

I would always wonder why no one's girlfriend experience was any different from being a wife. I question newlywed brides like a sponge wanting to soak up wisdom, because I believe God for marriage in my own life. "How is married life? Do things feel different?" Confused when 90% of the responses I would get were "Nothing has changed, it feels the same."

Why was this? How did you get this new position, this new role in life, and it not feel any different than when you were single? Most promotions or changes in life pull you out of your comfort zone. You must find balance, get a routine, figure out how to incorporate the new in your life. This happens on jobs, If I had to take a different route to work if there was construction going on. This happened after living in an apartment for ten years, and now owning a home. It took some getting used to, some readjustment. A lot of discomfort until I found balance. You mean to tell me, going from single to married feels no different? Somebody's not telling the truth.... Now I get it! This girlfriend position that we created, has taken away the excitement, expectation, responsibility, and work of what being a wife really is. And completely drained the freedom from us of being single. To be single (unmarried) means I don't have to submit to you, boyfriend. Cleaning and cooking for you, combining incomes with you, is not required of me, boyfriend. Having sex with you is really frowned upon, in the sight of the Lord and not required of me, boyfriend. I don't have to move you in, boyfriend. You don't get to drop me off and be gone in my car while I'm working, or I don't have to share my vehicle, boyfriend. What's mine isn't yours, boyfriend. We aren't one! I was never obligated to put up with bad attitudes and stubborn ways… Boyfriend.

"Wives, submit yourselves to your own husbands as you do to the Lord. For the husband is the head of the wife as Christ is the head of the church, his body of which he is the Savior. Now as the church submits to Christ, so also wives should submit to their husbands in everything."
Ephesians 5:22-24

    I had been over working myself and undervaluing the state in which I was in. I had gotten this all the way wrong. Once my eyes began to be opened, the desire for marriage changed. Not that I didn't want to still one day have a husband but I at this point I wanted to experience and enjoy something I hadn't taken the time to enjoy…. ME!

Chapter 6

"Destiny" (by: Tina Campbell)

Finding myself and learning myself has been a very timely process. As I'm typing this out, it's going on my sixth year of no boyfriend and me practicing celibacy, my second year since God revealed this word to me. I surrendered my will for who I wanted my husband to be a year ago. Eight months since my best friend expressed his love for me. Five months since God told my best friend I have to leave him behind. And about 7 or 8 days since that word has been confirmed for the third time and I'm being **OBEDIENT** to the voice of God.

I've been journaling and writing about this experience for the last six years. As I go back and read the entries, it amazes me, the growth, and how much my desires change. I had a lot of prayers about the man that I thought that I wanted. Prayers about the woman I wanted God to make me for him. Some entries of me complaining about this single life, others celebrating the victory of being single.

To experience the freedom that I have now, I had to keep it real with myself first. I had to come to terms with myself. I didn't want a husband at some point of my wait. I wanted to have "not guilty" sex. I wanted my flesh to be satisfied, with no conviction afterward. When you know better, the conviction is strong. I can remember when I was a girlfriend, sexually active, acting married, rolling over asking God for forgiveness, only to turn around and do it again the next day. That in itself tells you were the relationship with God was. To repent, but not really turn away. God wasn't pleased. I had to get that relationship right before trying to be with anyone else. Reading *Ezekiel 16* and how God called my actions worse than a prostitute, allowing myself to be with men other than my husband and I didn't even get payment made me disgusted with my own lustful sin. Not having physical sex, I still struggled with masturbation, convincing myself that it was okay, because I wasn't being active with an actual man. God still wasn't pleased. I would cry after each pleasurable moment, knowing good and well it wasn't right. I couldn't find scripture that said this specifically, so I tried to justify it. Yeah, I read about the brother Onan in *Genesis 38* that God killed. He married and spilled his seed on the ground. Because I enjoyed my sin I didn't feel as if that text applied to me because I wasn't a man. I just honestly wasn't ready to let go of the sin of masturbation. The word that convicted me and made me become conscious of my sin even in this area was *Hebrews 4:13* "Nothing in all creation is hidden from God's sight. Everything is uncovered and laid bare before the eyes of him to whom we must give account." This let me know that my secret addiction to pornography and masturbation that man couldn't see, that took place behind closed doors, God was very much aware of it. This sin I was able to hide for years. Being exposed to X-rated videos and magazines at the age of twelve, caused this secret addiction. As a child I found the magazines around the house. They were supposed to be hidden but this meddling twelve-year-old stumbled across them. Curiosity at an early age led to an adult addiction. God showed me that men with that same lustful spirit were attracted to the lustful spirit that lived in me. I repented and turned from my sin, and God delivered me from that.

"Therefore, you Israelites, I will judge each of you according to your own ways, declares the Sovereign Lord. Repent! Turn away from all your downfall. Rid yourselves of all the offenses you have committed and get a new heart and new spirit. Why will you die, people of Israel? For I take no pleasure in the death of anyone, declares the Sovereign Lord. Repent and live!" Ezekiel 18:30-32

"Finally, be strong in the Lord and in His mighty power. Put on the full armor of God, so that you might take your stand against the devil's schemes. For our struggle is not against flesh and blood, but against the rulers, against the authorities, against the powers of the dark world and against the spiritual forces of evil in the heavenly realms." – Ephesians 6:10-12

In the beginning when I was so frustrated about being single, I couldn't for the life of me understand why the Lord wouldn't let any of the men I encountered be the one. I could picture us together. I imagined in my head what our life would be like together. I'm not the only single woman that has experienced this. Keep it real! By the second or third phone call with some, we have a full vision of what we would like to happen with that person. At some point, until you find contentment with yourself, they all look like they could be the one.

    Keeping it real with myself I admitted things about myself, like the fact that I am easily annoyed. After so long I don't want to be bothered. I truly enjoy my own space. I hate the idea of answering to someone, being made to do anything doesn't sit well with me. I challenged a lot of what men say. I've either felt like I had to be a certain way, or men tried to make me be who they wanted me to be. Often feeling manipulated with the "if you love me, you'd do this or do that." Things that under normal circumstances I wouldn't subject myself to. But because I began to try to prove my love or fit their caliber, it caused me to step out of character. The majority of that was due to low self-esteem, and yeah, I wasn't in that low place anymore. It has taken me a long time to find my own identity, and I wasn't in the business of being anyone outside of who God called me to be.

    Coming to terms with my own truth and calling it out, realizing that slow fornication wasn't enough to want to be married, I accepted the fact that I already had the greatest husband.... Christ, until or if I'm blessed with a husband here on earth. Christ had already committed himself to being the head of my life.

"For your maker is your husband-the Lord Almighty is His name-the Holy One of Israel is your Redeemer; he is called the God of all the earth." - Isaiah 54:5

He knows me better than I know myself. He's a gentleman, provider, protector, and so much more. And He's faithful in doing so. I can trust Him and submit to Him. Before all of that, he's my friend.

"I no longer call you servants, because a servant does not know his master's business. Instead, I have called you friends, for everything I learned from my Father I have made known to you." - John 15:15

God knew I just wanted that 15-20-minute satisfaction, so my prayer for an earthly husband, he didn't answer. My motive was off. *"When you ask, you do not receive, because you ask with the wrong motives, that you may spend what you get on your pleasures" James 4:3.* I meant well wanting to be married in order to have sex considering, that's the only time God approves sex. But, it shouldn't be the foundation for marriage. God says I'm in my better. Don't desire sex so bad that you miss your better.

When I was a girlfriend, a cracked foundation had me fooled. Those few minutes felt like love that always helped to mend things back together, temporarily. Thinking that because we made each other feel good, that's all it took. I can remember being in "situation ships" with guys with different beliefs (unequally yoked). Purchasing a bible for one male companion wanting them to get to know the Lord. He appeared to have everything I desired from a man, except the relationship with God, thinking eventually, he would get that. We often feuded because we couldn't see eye to eye on certain things, not understanding the importance of a solid foundation, something everlasting. Sexual passion alone definitely isn't it.

"Anyone who listens to my teaching and follows it is wise, like a person who builds a house on solid rock. Through the rain comes in torrents and the floodwaters rise and the winds beat against that house, it won't collapse because it is built on bedrock. But anyone who hears my teaching and doesn't obey it is foolish, like a person who builds a house on sand. When the rains and the flood come and the winds beat against that house, it will collapse with a mighty crash." Matthew 7:24-27

"Do not be yoked together with unbelievers. For what do righteousness and wickedness have in common? Or what fellowship can light have with darkness?" 2 Corinthians 6:14

"Do not be misled: "Bad company corrupts good character."

1Corinthians 15:3

Chapter 7

"Moving Forward" (by: Israel Houghton)

It's a blessing to be free from the things of your past! When I say I'm free, it doesn't mean all these things just went away. I can't erase the memory of some of the trauma, although I've tried too, because PTSD is real. However, I'm free from allowing the things of my past to control me anymore. I no longer live in silence or shame, understanding that who and where I am now is only evidence of God's healing power, and deliverance. The freedom I can't describe, you should actually experience it for yourself.

I was "to death do us part" with men who weren't my husband. I was loyal with no commitment on their end. I made up my mind one day I was going to write myself a singles decree. A decree making me commit to where I was and not focusing on where I wanted to be so much. I didn't want to miss the state in which I was in.

Singles Decree

I decree to enjoy my better (me). I decree to no longer mourn over the Saul's in my life that God rejected as King. Those who left me, let them go. I will demonstrate love towards me, daily. I will love me the way God loves me. I will boldly ask, and it will be given unto me. I will keep the commandments of the Lord. I will live a life of purity and avoid sexual immorality. I will sanctify my body. I will love with my heart. I will live in my truth. I am free indeed.

This was a vow I decided to make to myself. Since I was going to be here, just me and the Lord, I might as well be good to me. I knew He would be. How I treat myself will dictate how others feel they can treat me. Why not set the standard high?

Truth has been my pathway to this freedom. Even after getting back out there trying this dating thing again. I had changed, but some of the same men were out there. Wanting to get what they could, from whomever they could get it from. With my new-found wisdom, I tried my best to avoid this type. I would interact with some that appeared interested, but once they learned I wasn't having sex, they only wanted to deal with me on their time and on their terms, until I caught on to what was happening, I was still asking "Lord, what's up?" I decided to switch it up. Let me let them know out the gate, that this is what it is. If they choose to leave or stay, they can do so now. Some legit guys, they just weren't for me. I would find myself entangled in some of the same behavior. Not having sex but allowing these men to touch, feel, fondle me. God wasn't pleased.

During this process, I had to learn what was appropriate and inappropriate. *"God searches the actions of man" - Jeremiah 17:10*. This convicted me to realizing something as simple as, spending the night wasn't pleasing in God's sight. This is one of the bad habits that somewhere along the line, I picked up and made ok. It's what I always did with other men in the past, it's what I saw growing up. Even not being sexually involved with each other. I could preach about waiting all I wanted, but if my actions weren't lining up with my talk, men would believe something else was capable of happening. When I took notice of the mixed message I was sending, this caused me to want to do better. I had to undo a lot of things that I would naturally begin to do when I decided I was going to be with someone. I kissed, rubbed and touched until I realized I was playing with fire by putting myself in the way of temptation. Now I've vowed that no one is to receive such intimate behavior unless they were my spouse. The Lord has shown me that each time I allow a man to touch me, that isn't my husband, I allow virtue to leave me. Virtue that belongs only to God, or a husband. I wasn't designed to feed, nourish, groom, or multiply with a boyfriend. I had to learn to set boundaries and unlearn worldly habits. Easier said than done. Somewhere life taught me that love was to give up my body.

"When I wrote to you before, I told you not to associate with people who indulge in sexual sin. But I wasn't talking about unbelievers who

indulge in sexual sin, or are greedy, or cheat people, or worship idols. You would have to leave this world to avoid people like that. I meant that you are not to associate with anyone who claims to be a believer[a] yet indulges in sexual sin, or is greedy, or worships idols, or is abusive, or is a drunkard, or cheats people. Don't even eat with such people. It isn't my responsibility to judge outsiders, but it certainly is your responsibility to judge those inside the church who are sinning. God will judge those on the outside; but as the Scriptures say, "You must remove the evil person from among you." 1Corinthians 5:9-13 NLT

"Or do you not know that the wrongdoers will not inherit the kingdom of God? Do not be deceived: Neither the sexual immortal nor the idolaters nor adulterers nor men who men who have sex with men nor thieves nor greedy nor drunkards nor slanders nor swindlers will inherit the kingdom of God." 1 Corinthians 6:9-10

The times that I came up against the possibility of having sex, the Lord kept me. The Lord, and me remembering how powerful sex is. I would think about how I use to feel, powerless. Like I had no control and couldn't walk away from the men that I laid down with. You know how it is. That one that you know you need to leave alone but can't because he got you all the way together. His ability to please you physically, caused him to have you mentally. Convincing myself over and over again that I could operate as a man, be sexually involved and not get attached, sooner or later finding myself attached anyhow. That thought alone of me being that tore up about somebody made my "no" stronger and stronger. Being free from the trap of pre-marital sex. I never want to be so deeply connected to any man at that capacity, that isn't my husband.

"He who finds a wife finds what is good and receives favor from the Lord." Proverbs 1:22 NIV

Once it registered that I was the good thing that brought about favor and that I had to already be a wife in order to be found, my perspective changed. I really was working too hard trying to find a man. When in reality, they should have been trying to find me. Now, instead of getting myself caught up in a lie that men are more than what they are in my life, I choose to continue my theme of keeping it real with me. I do the opposite of what you hear most people say. Instead of deleting or blocking contacts from my phone, I started naming men based off my experience with them. This is my way of reminding myself who I'm dealing with. Women are attracted to what they hear. If the wrong man gets on the phone saying the right words, I would end up right where I started. This was my way of protecting myself. I have in my contacts as of right now: He's bored, Strictly Client, I don't need another friend,

Comfortable where he is, Lust not Love, God healed you from this, and Shoulda Coulda Woulda. Each name to remind myself of what position they have in my life, if any, and their real intentions with me. When they call I don't get wrapped up in their feel-good words about what they should have done, or plan to do. Like the infamous Maya Angelou said, "When someone shows you who they are, believe them the first time."

Chapter 8

"I am what you see" (by: William Murphy)

When you come to terms with the fact that God has such a bigger plan for you and your life, then the rest of the world's blueprint. You think different, dream different, and move differently. You dream bigger when you understand that God has the power to control all things!

Growing up, you often refer to someone living the "American Dream!" This American way consists of having the house, the spouse, children, career, the white picket fence, and occasionally a dog or two. For a long time, that dream was my dream. That dream was embedded in me. The family that checked off on most or all of these things, was admired. Education, career, family, and nowadays, it doesn't necessarily have to be in that order. You hear chase your dreams, when truly the dream chaser isn't nearly celebrated as much as the one who appears "qualified" because they have all of these things. Especially when your dream doesn't resemble everyone else's.

Once I began to change my way of thinking, and my motives were checked, I realized the American dream wasn't big enough for me. There is more in me than to just settle for what everyone else is aiming for. After all, *"I'm made fearfully and wonderfully,"* Psalm 139:14. Unique! So why in the world should my life mimic America's dream? Why should

I allow limitations on what my life should look like, simply because it's never been done this way before?

America tells me by now I should be married, or at least have had one child. America says "you ain't talking to nobody?" America wants to know what "title" any companion of the opposite sex carries, especially if you're both single. America wants to know what's wrong with you if you aren't with anyone, by now. I'm asking America, "what's wrong with you, and your small ways of thinking?'

When I began to change my prayer. "God show me your vision for my life. Allow your dream to become my dream. I know your vision for my life is far greater." God showed me so much that was available to me.

"For I know the plans I have for you," declares the Lord, "plans to prosper you and not to harm you, plans to give you hope and a future. Then you will call on me and come to pray to me, and I will listen to you. You will seek me and find me when you seek me with your heart. I will be found by you," declares the Lord, "and will bring you back from captivity. I will gather you from all the nations and places where I have banished you," declares the Lord, " and will bring you back to the place from which I carried you into exile." - Jerimiah 29:11-14

Sorry America, not all of my accomplishments are going to include a husband. In one of my journal entries I told you all about, I planned to purchase a house. I was so specific and detailed in what I wanted that purchasing to look like. I live to this day by *"write the vision make it plain upon tablets, that he may run that readeth."* Habakkuk 2:2

Detailed to the point of knowing what I wanted to save for a down payment, how much I wanted as a mortgage payment, how many bedrooms, what I needed to save monthly for this to happen, and where my credit score needed to be to make this possible. In this planning, I also wrote that, who I thought at the time would be my husband, and myself, would continue to live in my apartment, until we were able to afford this house. With all this planning and after a year of looking, I finally found the house for me. Revelation came that what I was asking for wasn't what I was looking for. Approved for one amount, but I petitioned the Lord for a house that fell in a rate asking for something else. I was able to get everything I was praying and planning for, for $30,000 less than what I was approved by the bank for.

My written-out plan to getting my first home came to pass, other than me doing it with a man. God honored my request and added a bit of his flavor to it. Which in the long run, made things better. He acted and served as the head of the house and led and guided me through the entire process. He surrounded me with people that had already went through the home buying process and made it that much easier for me. He encouraged me in times of distress. When fear crept in, he sent someone with the right words to uplift me. I walked in that lawyer's office and signed those papers with only my signature on them, to my house. God did it! This is no jab at anyone who purchased their first home with their spouse, that's a beautiful thing. I'm glad it was your husband. This is to encourage that woman feeling like she's stuck where she is until she gets a husband. Not true girl!

That's what I believed, not that I couldn't. I've always been a go getter. An extremely hard worker, at anything I do. But I never understood why I would even need a house with no spouse or kids. That's the lie I believed, that I wouldn't be able to afford it without a man. Nope, I'm not the first to ever do it, but I'll share what some women won't, my journey.

Being single, self-employed, with no dependents, people think you're rich. Especially the IRS. Uncle Sam wants every dime that is owed to him. Being self-employed most people think I just make up numbers and get away with not paying taxes at all. The truth of the matter is, they're probably right. This would be the case, if I didn't know Jesus. Cause honey, those tax bills in April... Writing that check is never fun. Being OBEDIENT *"So give back to Caesar what is Caesar's, and to God what is God's." Matthew 22:21,* and reporting my full income, allowed me to be approved by the bank for my house, with just my income listed on the loan. Had I tried to finagle the system, I could have missed my blessing. The day before my original closing date I got a phone call from the mortgage lender, saying I couldn't close because the IRS hadn't filed my taxes yet. I, like most tax payers that owe, waited until the very last day to file. Who's ever in a rush to pay them? I always do a paper claim when I file, because again, who cares? You owe! I forgot to sign my tax forms that I submitted, but I sent the payment owed. The IRS cashed my check but returned my forms to be signed. By the time I put them back in the mail, it was now time to close on the house. Six to eight weeks is all they would say when calling to see if there was any way to expedite the filing process. The seller of the house was about to pull out and put the house back on the market if he had to wait six to eight weeks. When I mentioned to the mortgage company that the IRS had already cashed my check, they asked if I could verify it. I faxed a copy of the check, and documents where the funds had come out of my checking account to the mortgage company. The underwriter approved my closing, without having to wait the six to eight weeks. God is good, and OBEDIENCE is always better than sacrifice.

"Now unto him who is able to do immeasurably more than all we ask or imagine, according to his power that is at work within us." Ephesians 3:20

This scripture continues to blow my mind. It say's He (God) is able to do more than I can imagine. That's crazy to me, because I know how big my imagination is. My imagination tends to run wild and think big. My mind is constantly racing. I've pictured myself doing all type of things, and you mean to tell my God can put together something that is greater than that? I want that dream! God's dream!

Being a girlfriend, my boyfriend's dreams became my dreams. I put off what I wanted to do in life to promote the boyfriend's dreams and aspiration. Why was this? I made what they wanted out of life a priority over my own goals. Here I am making goals to buy houses, cars, promoting them and their business, or whatever it was that they did. Then when it didn't work I would experience what I assume divorce feels like. Why did I waste that unnecessarily traumatic experience on a boyfriend? Furthermore, I was investing my knowledge, ideas, and worth into men who had no right to me. God called women to be helpers to our husbands. It's my husband that can deposit a vision or dream into me, and I help bring it into fruition, not a boyfriend.

Getting rid of the actual boyfriend and the baggage that came with them was good. Growing older and building a career feels good. I'm still believing God to bless me with a husband. It never registered to me before that being a girlfriend isn't just something you are, it's a mentality as well. A mentality that is so concerned with what others think of you and what they believe you should be doing with your life. Submitting to other's will for my life. Though I haven't been in a committed relationship with a man for a number of years, God showed me I operated in relationships with family, my business partner, and other friendships, still as a girlfriend. Allowing a lot of the same circumstances from the past relationships, in these relationships, getting the same end result. God couldn't send my husband as long as I had a girlfriend mentality. I was in a business partnership with a female friend as co-owner of a salon. Originally when asked to partner I said no and shared with her that I thought God wanted her and her spouse to run the business together. God never spoke to me saying to go. As she continued getting the salon together, my answer hadn't changed because I hadn't heard from God.

Things started happening at the salon I was working at, at the time, that made me question if I was to stay or go. I believe God was trying to tell me something, but I now see where I never stopped to ask Him what that something was exactly. I took my focus off God and started focusing on what people thought. I assumed and listened to the voices of everyone else to tell me how great of an opportunity partnering would be, and I was convinced that this was what God had for me. Once I joined her, things that she was having trouble finding, started coming together. It made me really believe this was a part of Gods doing. Even if God was telling me to go, I never stopped to ask Him. I now see where I trusted the voice of God's people, over the voice of God. Growing in a relationship with Christ, God has always given me His word to back up whatever He was telling me to do. God sends people to confirm his plan, but they aren't the author of His plan for my life. I went to where it made sense to me, and man, and our small thinking. I never sought after a word from the Lord to confirm it. God blessed me while I was there and allowed me to stay for a little while. But I still had to live out His will for my life. Four years later I get a text in the middle of the night that my friend no longer wanted to be my business partner, and a lease was already signed on another building, and I was welcome to come along, if I liked, but no longer be her partner. She and her spouse were now going to run the business. Several emotions went through me when reading this text message. In the moment I wasn't mad at all. Prior to receiving this text, she and I had been considering relocating the business together that we currently had. We both originally agreed that it wasn't a move that we needed to make, because we hadn't built up the brand name we currently had. People knew her, and they knew me, but they didn't know the salon name. And for me, fear had crept in at the thought of relocating, not wanting to take on any extra responsibility. After seeing the building, we decided to be in prayer about what God wanted us to do. While in prayer about both the salon and the house, I heard God say relocate but was seeking clarity on which move He wanted me to make. I would ask my business partner if she thought this was something we should just step out on faith and go after, never knowing a decision was already made.

When you are in tune with the Lord, he gives you warning. God had shown me in a dream days before this text, the name of another salon. I had no clue why God had the name of another friend's salon all in my dream. Eight months before all this had happened, the friend with the salon called and said God showed her us with a partnership. She said she didn't know what it meant but she would be praying. My response back when she called and after the dream, was that God hadn't shown me that, and if God wanted me there, He would have to do it. My loyalty was with the friend I was partnered with. Whelp, God did it, and it hurt. It hurt because I had breakfast with my business partner earlier the day the text was sent. I shared my dreams and vision for the business and nothing was ever mentioned. This dream and this message were a clear sign of what God wanted me to do, and where he wanted me to go.

My family was disappointed at how things went down, but more disappointed that I didn't respond how they thought that I should have. Sometimes walking this Christian walk, the hardest thing is not responding how your flesh wants you to, or how you were once accustomed to. My friend that's like a sister and I, when we have to turn the other cheek and not respond, we say, "I just got jumped!" That's what it feels like when you have to be the bigger person and can't fight back in your flesh. You feel like you got punked out, but I've learned that

I have to show Jesus love in all things. That doesn't mean I don't get upset., Heck, Jesus was no punk, he flipped over tables. I know I'm held accountable for my actions. Plus, I wanted to pass this test from God. I didn't want to have to repeat this test again. I knew God had a reason, but why this painful?

    I began asking God to let me stay at the location we were currently renting and allow me to open my own salon. He gave me, "*and no one pours new wine into old wine skins. Otherwise, the new wine will burst the skins; the wine will run out and the wineskins will be ruined*"- *Luke 5: 37.* I knew where I was supposed to go. Even in my knowing I wasn't happy about it and God told me I had to go because "*as iron sharpens Iron, so one person sharpens another*"- *Proverbs 27:17.* Devastated at the idea that this happened, I cried out to God asking him to allow me to birth something of my own. Doing hair was all I thought I had, and that's all people had seen me do. Pride told me to go find my own building and start a salon. The following week I went out and looked at three different buildings and wasn't satisfied with any of them. My male best friend sent me a song "Surrender", by Psalmist Raine. We do that often, send each other YouTube videos of songs and sermons. He said it reminded him of me when I lead worship. I hadn't talked to him, so he didn't know what was going on with the salon and how this song was ministering to me. Listening to the words of the song made me realize I had to surrender my own will and go where God was sending me. Regardless of if it made sense to me or not. God told me I had to let my friend know by that Saturday that I was coming. I was OBEDIENT and called her late that Saturday night to let her know that I was going to be coming to rent a booth at her salon. She was very understanding to my hesitation about wanting to move, and my now severe trust issues. The next day while sitting in church, I received a text message from my still business partner asking me to call her when I got a chance. I called after service and was asked if I knew what I wanted to do. I told her I was going to my friend's salon. She asked if I could be out by July. It was now the last week in May. I was in the process of closing on my home that was located close to the salon that I was currently at. When my business partner and I originally talked after the text message was sent about the move over the phone, September or October was the potential moving date thrown out there, which is where my attempt to try to get my own salon came from. I knew I could do it in a three to four-month time frame. Apparently, God was accelerating this thing, which is why he told me to tell my friend the day before that I was coming. Thank God I surrendered and was OBEDIENT.

    Transitioning was HARD. New home, new salon, this man is now pursuing me, and friendships were changing. My life shifted all at once, and it took a while to adjust to two places at the same time. Working and living out of boxes was no fun at all, and took a lot longer to unpack than I expected. During this timeframe, I kept pulling on God. I knew there had to be more for my life than this. I began to read books on faith; Think and Grow Rich and Jump by Steve Harvey. I listened to motivational speeches by Denzel Washington and Will Smith and did more self-evaluating. Trying to understand what was happening, what God was doing, and trying to prevent myself from slipping into depression. What I knew as my world and what was comfortable to me had all been taken away from me. Slightly confused because the last time God stripped everything from me, I downgraded. This time, each area of my life was being upgraded. I didn't see becoming a booth renter again as an upgrade at first, but soon learned to appreciate the position, because it allowed me to focus more on getting things at home situated, and it helped devote more time to doing things I wanted to do for me. I had been gracefully broken. The books, speeches and a lot of prayer helped me to remember, I never wanted to do hair. This was the thing that God brought me to. I fell in love with the talent that he gave me and making money from doing it. I never wanted to own a salon that I worked in.

    I heard God saying, "go back to the well." The well is the place that I experienced God for myself. The place He offered His living water. The place he revealed my truth to me. I had to go back to the beginning and remember my dream to write. I had to separate my talent of doing hair from my gift to teach. Learning what my gift was, helped me to feel like I had purpose again. I had to go back to the place where God showed me to write this book back in December of 2016, when I ended up in the hospital for pneumonia. I don't get sick that often, but when I do it's bad. It had never been this bad to have a four-night hospital stay. I had rode to Nashville the Sunday before with some friends. We went to a church that we wanted to visit and to do a little shopping at their outlet mall. The Pastor at the church we attended spoke over the house that "moving into the twelfth month, God is putting things into order. God is saying immediately." That was Sunday. By Tuesday I was sick. I went into work thinking nothing of it. Half way through I had to cancel all scheduled clients for the day. Wednesday night I was admitted into the hospital. At first I was too sick to process what was happening. I soon realized God had me in this place because He needed to reveal some things and needed my full attention. Once I figured out what was going on, my physical body felt fine. I was at peace and had no pain. On the inside God was doing some cleansing. My doctor asked me what I had been doing. The entire right lung was filled with pneumonia. I had to have a scope procedure done that required them to put me to sleep. They went in through my mouth with a scope, down through my lungs and broke up the bacteria.

    This hospital visit caused my relationship with my mother and I to shift. I talked to her about things that I had never voiced before. Hearing the words, "I love you" for the first time from her at the age of thirty-two. I always knew my mother loved me. She has sacrificed so much for my brothers and myself, especially my older brother and I, being she was a teenage mother. She expressed her love by her actions and not her words, which is how I learned to express my love, by doing and not necessarily saying. I knew she loved me by the way she took care of me. As I grew older, I gained understanding that her discipline, those whooping's, were out of love too. It was something about hearing those word for the first time that brought joy, peace, and made me feel like she was proud of the woman that I had become. Raised to be so independent and tough, and taught to learn how to figure it out on your own, left no room for the women in my family to be sensitive. The words "I love you" were foreign in my family. Words that were rarely said to each other that often, or at all. The hospital visit served purpose.

God told me using *Romans 4* "Your good deeds are great, but they didn't lead to His righteousness, faith does. God said put people down and walk in faith in what I said you can do. Write the book, buy your house, go to school, become a wife, make the album, have a world-wide ministry." Nothing about hair. I was guilty of being a caregiver to everyone else and neglecting myself. God said no more. "Believe me for your dream." It was time. You are Released!

Resting in this fresh word from Heaven I got out of the hospital, and the next day went and enrolled in Simmons College of Kentucky. I had been talking about wanting to take a semester of Music Theory with one of the musicians at the church I attend, believing it would be a real asset and help to sharpen my gift of singing and make things make sense musically. God showed me favor. I was able to get enrolled directly into music theory, a vocal training class, aural skills, and the required class for all freshmen in college, Pathways to Success. A bit more than what I bargained for, but I was willing to make the necessary sacrifices. I wasn't approved for any type of grants for school, and because Simmons is a school that wants you to graduate debt free, they don't accept student loans. Which meant I was going to be paying out of pocket. No, it wasn't something I had budgeted for but knew I had to be OBEDIENT to the voice of God. The school gave me so many days to come up with a financial plan to get school paid for before I could enroll. Monthly payments were an option, payment amounts that were going to cause me to be on an extremely tight budget for the next five months.

    I had returned back to work and made a few changes to how I was going to be operating my business, determined that school was going to happen. I was overjoyed about this new promising endeavor. Talking school over with one of my clients that is a teacher, she told me that her family had a scholarship with Simmons. That each semester they grant it to someone and I could use it toward my tuition. God again was making a way. When attending the meeting to set up the payment arrangement, I was advised that because I was taking four classes, that qualified me to put my current student loan payments on deferment. Meaning I wouldn't have to pay my current student loan payments as long as I was enrolled in school. My monthly payments after the scholarship was applied, were the same amount that I was already adjusted to paying each month for student loans. What I calculated and thought was going to overextend me, God had already worked it out that nothing would change. I was able to enjoy my experience at school, not being concerned with how I was going to get things paid for each month. Each one of my classes helped to stretch me musically. My Pathway to success class required tons of writing. This class helped to ignite the fire the I had for writing again. Getting positive feedback from my professor on my papers helped build my confidence when it came time to finish up this book.

It may not seem like much to anyone else, but I made two A's and two B's that semester. I'll celebrate the small things. On the very last day of class, after I had taken my last final, I left school and found the house that I purchased. I now see where God is lining everything up that he told me during my "well" experience.

During the birthing process of this book and healing from the loss of a business and friend, God showed me I still had the same girlfriend mentality, attaching myself to someone else's stuff and making it my own. It now makes complete sense why my business partner and I had to separate. I could no longer be a part of her journey. I had gotten too comfortable in something that didn't belong to me. Operating in someone else's disobedience. The dream for that salon belonged to her and her husband. She wouldn't be able to fully flourish in her dream as long as I was attached to it. God had to get me to a place that I could have something that belonged to me. I had to dream again and create a new journey for myself. God's Journey! One that didn't and couldn't include everyone that I would have taken with me. I say to America, you can have your dream, it hasn't quite worked out in my favor. I will follow Christ's dream for me., He has a better track record than America. I'm building my own brand.

"Therefore, my dear brothers and sisters, stand firm. Let nothing move you. Always give yourselves fully to the work of the Lord, because you know that your labor in the Lord is not in vain." 1Coritnthians 15:58

Chapter 9

"It was Necessary" (by: Fantasia)

Here I am tapping into other gifts that God deposited in me. Away from all the noise, alone to be with Christ, allowing Him to pull out his very best in me, seeing new visions and new possibilities every day. Literally feeling God's healing and understanding why all the separations had to happen. I was robbing everyone that I enabled an opportunity to get to know God for themselves. Robbing myself by having a girlfriend's mentality and submitting to anyone other than Christ. OBEDIENCE is a choice I choose knowing that God always knows what's best for me. Even when fear creeps up and I don't understand what God is doing. The fear of God and love of God makes me choose God. God is the most consistent being in my life. He's faithful, that's why I say Yes to God's will. I don't know why I would have ever trusted someone else with me.

"Being confident in this, that he who began a good work in you will carry it on to completion until the day of Christ Jesus." Philippians 1:6

"The Sovereign Lord is my strength he makes my feet of a deer, he enables me to tread on the heights." Habakkuk 3:19

"Love the Lord your God and keep his requirements, his decrees, his laws, and his commands always." Deuteronomy 11:1

To my sisters screaming where's my Boaz. Let's examine the story of Ruth in the bible. Revelation came that, I wanted to be a Ruth and gain a Boaz but didn't want to leave my family behind like Ruth did. *Ruth 1.* She left what was comfortable to her, to go to unfamiliar territory to get something different. This wasn't just the family I was birthed into, but the one I created, and all the things of my past, all the hurt and bad experiences that had me so guarded. One part of me idolized marriage, another part of me became afraid of the idea of marriage, because I was afraid of losing myself and losing freedom. Thinking that my freedom came from my singleness. *1 Timothy 2: 5-6* tells us that Christ Jesus purchased freedom for everyone. Not just the single, everyone. When reading this, it helped me to understand, my freedom was bought on Calvary, and as long as I was connected to Jesus, I'm free to be who I am. Regardless if I stay single or decide to marry. I didn't experience freedom in my previous relationships because Christ wasn't in them. My lack of identity in those relationships was due to my lack of relationship with God. As long as I remain in Christ, I will remain Janee'. I will carry my identity. The titles added along the journey, can't stop my freedom. The husband that God has for me will accept me, love me, just as I am. Ruth also allowed Naomi's God to become her God. I surrounded myself with Naomi women, that helped to disciple me along this walk with Christ. Until I got with Jesus, The Son of God *John 3:16*. The truth and life God, to get to one you must know the other God *John 14:6*. The Alpha and Omega God *Revelation22:13*. The Resurrected God *Luke 24:6-7*. All Knowing God *Matthew 10:30*. Holds all power God *Luke 1:37*. The Living Water God *John 4:14*. I would have never got to this place. Place of peace, healing, and bearing good fruit.

Boaz noticed Ruth when she went to glean(working). *Ruth 2*. Instead of going out, trying to be seen I'll continue to do the work the Lord has called me to. OBEDIENT to God and under the authority of The Shepherd of the house, my Pastor *Ephesians 4:11*. More than ever, *Matthew 6:33* takes relevance in my life. *"But seek first his kingdom and his righteousness, and all these things will be given to you as well."* The more I seek God, the more God continues to reveal himself. He has taken notice of me and found out who I am. I will continue to sit at the threshing floor at the feet of Jesus. *Ruth 3*. The place that later, Martha was told, was the right position to be in *Luke 10:41*. There are answers to all my questions at the feet of Jesus.

Accepting the guardian-redeemers that felt like I was too much of a risk to redeem for themselves and receive the one willing to endure all of me. *Ruth 4*. There were men that appeared to fit the qualifications to be the one. As decent as these men were, I had to learn there is Free will. The Lord is a gentleman and doesn't force anything on anyone. We all have a choice to choose. I had to be willing to let go of the one's that had the opportunity presented to them but weren't willing to choose. My God has gladly married me and deposited in me.

I'm finally giving birth. *I'm no one's girlfriend & OBEDIENCE got me here.*

This book was formed out of OBEDIENCE. Back in 2015 I had a friend that had a Go Fundme account going around on Facebook. Collecting money to go on a trip out of town, for an opportunity that she wanted to take advantage of. My Facebook page was deactivated at the time, but I heard about it. I soon received a text in a group message that she was looking for donations. I knew I would give but hadn't determined the amount yet. One night I was headed to the gym, and before I went in, I heard God tell me to go make up the difference of what is owed for her to go on the trip. I cried real tears thinking, "Lord what?" I had so much I wanted to do with that money. And even if I decided to do nothing with it, I liked the idea of having it there as security. Knowing I had to be OBEDIENT I made the payment and learned a very valuable lesson. God is my security. He provides. I say to myself to this day "trust God more than you trust your money." Knowing that my income can only get me so far. Standing on what Jesus said, *"with man this looks impossible, but with God all things are possible." Matthew 19:26* There are no limits to what can be done, with God. When making the payment I did it as anonymous, not needing credit or accolades for what God was doing. *"But when you give to the needy, do not let your left hand know what your right hand is doing, so that your giving may be in secret. Then your Father, who sees what is done in secret, will reward you." Matthew 6:3-4.* Other's couldn't see who made the donation, but my friend could on her end. She called me crying saying thank you, and in return she wanted to do a painting for me. I reassured her she owed me nothing. She wanted to do it as her way of saying thank you. Months go by, and when she finally had time to create the painting, she texts me and tells me to send her about six to seven things that I want out of life. She writes those things on the canvas before painting over it. Among several other things named I texted back, "Author." She responded surprised, saying she didn't know that I write, and asked what type of book I had thought about writing. I explained my desires. She responds again and says "you know the trip you funded me for was to teach me how to write a book. I can help you when you're ready."

NOBODY BUT GOD. I mean, I know he's God and can do all things. Yet it still amazes me when I see God flex His hand in my life. He had me pay for her to go, for information that I would soon be needing. He knew what was around the corner. My friend has been able to help me every step of the way, using what she learned or pointing me in the direction of other resources. It was hard trusting her at first with something so precious to me. Like a new mother birthing her first child, I needed to know it was safe in her hands. Not because of anything she did, but the last experience partnering with someone, caused fear and anxiety to kick in. I had to constantly remind myself through this process that God put us together, not man. It was ok to trust her. I had to push past my fear and trust God, or this would just be words in a Word document.

Chapter 10

"I'm Getting Ready" (by: Tasha Cobb Leonard)

The night after I got the text of what felt like the end of my world, I cried and cried and cried. Tired of being such and such's auntie, oh boy's girl, dudes sister, and a friend of a friend. I wanted something that belonged to me. I logged on to Instagram that night after months of not being on there. Just looking for something, not sure what. I hear Tasha Cobb doing a studio session for her latest album. Singing, "I'm getting ready to see something I've never seen. God's about to blow my mind." I cried myself to sleep playing these words over and over. Still in tears a week later I cried out to the Lord like Hannah in *1 Samuel*, asking God to allow me to birth something of my own. My Pastor preached a sermon the next day May 21, 2017 entitled "You done started something." He came from *2nd Kings 4:8-10 & 15-17*. He professed in his sermon that God says just sit down for a minute, I'm making room for you to rest for a minute, and this time next year, you will have a child! I stood on that word, and every word since for guidance and direction.

Hearing clearly from God at times, other times struggling, God is showing me in this new season that he won't come the way he has before. He is allowing me to get to know Him on a new level. A fresh revelation came as I was driving on the expressway. Headed to a place I had never been before, I used my GPS. I knew where I was going but had no clue how to get there. All I knew is that I was to take the Breckinridge exit. Driving in that direction, exiting the ramp, I was depending on the GPS to say to me if it was exit A or B. The GPS was silent. Looking at the illustration of the live map, the arrow was showing me that I passed up my exit. I was now headed in the wrong direction. Irritated, I began to cry in my car, about three other things had went wrong this day, so missing my exit had put the cherry on top of the cake. Also, disappointed feeling like this was what I was experiencing from God. I was listening but couldn't hear him speaking. Within seconds of me missing the exit and getting irritated. I realized that even though the GPS hadn't spoken to me to tell me which direction to go in, on my screen it said take Breckinridge South at the top but I never paid attention to it, because I was focusing on getting the direction the way that I had grown accustomed to. This time around direction was given but in a different way. God has been operating in a completely different way in my life, causing me to be stretched and to be watchful, he's always with me guiding me along the way. After reaching my destination, I turned my GPS back on to help get me back to the expressway. Now trying to listen to music, the GPS was still talking in my car, now over powering the song I was trying to listen to. I went to turn the GPS off, because I had now reached a familiar place, and knew my way back home. I didn't need the GPS anymore. God showed me again, that that was exactly how I was doing him. I ask for his direction and guidance, but once I reached a place that I felt like "I got this," I would put Him down. When clearly, I need Him all the way. A couple of days later I had to use my GPS again to go somewhere. Remembering the lesson from days before, I knew it would behoove me to use my navigation system the entire way through. As I was leaving my house the voice on the system told me that there was a six- minute delay that I would be approaching due to a crash, but I was still on the fastest route. I couldn't do anything but laugh. This confirmed how important it is to submit all my plans and dreams with the Lord at the very beginning. He gives warning, alerts ahead of time to let us know of hurdles and delays that we will face, that we can't see. Prior to this valuable life lesson, I went for a consultation for a breast reduction on January 9, 2018. I came up with a wonderful financial plan to make it happen. With a goal of taking off work the entire month of July 2018 to heal, returning right before school starts back. When I submitted my plan to the Lord, He said, "no, it was going to put me in the rear." I'm not quite sure right now what that means. But I will be OBEDIENT to the "no." God's knows what's best and see's ahead. Only he knows what will happen in July.

    I'm no one's girlfriend & OBEDIENCE got me here! One thing's for certain I'll remain Committed and Submitted unto the Lord all the days of my life. I'm grateful that *"the Lord is my shepherd, I lack nothing" – Psalm 23:1.* I'll let God do the deciding as to when I'm ready for a husband.

January 28, 2018 at 1:30am God whispered, "you're now experiencing your healing." Confirmed later in the day with a preached word from *Luke17:11-19*. Referencing the ten with leprosy as years instead of people. The last nine years, and now in this case chapters, didn't say thank you. But the one, chapter ten, will come back and say thank you! I'm currently living my chapter ten. I don't know what happens in this chapter. It's new, I'm healed, and whole. I've never been here before. So far, I have been practicing self-love, dealing with the insecurities that I have been holding on to. I prayed and asked God to teach me how to love my best friend well. See, I'm a handful, and a bit spoiled at times. I don't always have the best attitude. My best friend has always managed to love me through it. I want to be able to do the same for him in return. God showed me, I can't love him well because I don't love myself well. *"Love your neighbor as yourself" - Matthew 22:39.* I'm always thinking if I were a size smaller, didn't wear glasses, had a smaller nose or bigger butt then I would be loveable. And I'm just really hard on myself, not always extending myself grace, or allowing myself to fail. These things don't matter to my best friend, more importantly, they don't matter to God. I'm currently working on not allowing them to matter to me.

I've partnered with two ladies from my church and started a company J'adore Unlimited. J'adore means *love* in French. The idea is for it to be a brand that supports all things that we love and are passionate about. Our first event "Let it burn" stemmed off the vision and movement of practicing self-love first. My best friend had originally done the "let it burn" with the youth at our church. I decided to host a session amongst friends, simply because I wanted to deal with my own stuff. My desire to want to see others free, made me take it to Facebook to see who would come if I hosted. The response surprised me. It ended up being all women that wanted to participate. To make sure everyone that attended was comfortable, I told my best friend I would do the session, instead of having him to come in and do so. He gave guidance on what was to be done. Through prayer, God gave me scripture to back this up. The event brought out twenty women that sit in the cold around a fire pit for two and a half hours. Sharing their own insecurities, throwing them in the fire and no longer carrying or allowing those things to hold them back from seeing themselves the way God sees them. These women encouraged one another and were able to hear each other's perspectives on life. On my own personal time, I'm constantly throwing things in the fire. Fears and self-doubt. Anything that goes against what God says about me.

As I come to a close in this book, I went back to Georgia for the Demonstrat8 conference. This time God didn't allow me to go alone.

God told me I had to do what was uncomfortable to me, in order to become what he is calling me to be. Being OBEDIENT, I went, and stayed with three friends that I have never traveled with before. I didn't even get to drive, which is unusual for me, being I'm the designated driver when I have traveled in the past. I went with great expectations and was blessed! I entered a place of worship that I've never experienced before, entered the Holy of Holies and received my gift of tongue. In complete humility I cried before the Lord, remembering the last time I encountered his language. This time I was experiencing it during intimacy with the Lord. Returning from the conference, I was confident in doing the work God has called me too. Understanding that the same grace that falls on the leaders of the conference falls on me. I'm ready to work even closer with my Pastor to take the ministry to a higher level.

Each day in this chapter of my life is different., It's new and so am I! I don't know what tomorrow brings. I'm still writing this chapter! I'm living life out of routine, based on no one else's concerns but the Lords. Standing on the word that he's given me in this season.

"Moses my servant is dead. Now then, you and all these people, get ready to cross the Jordan River into the land I am about to give to them- to the Israelites. I will give you every place where you set your foot, as I promised Moses. Your territory will extend from the desert to Lebanon, and from the great river, the Euphrates- all the Hittite country- to the Mediterranean Sea in the west. No one will be able to

stand against you all the days of your life. As I was with Moses, so I will be you; I will never leave you nor forsake you. Be strong and courageous, because you will lead these people to inherit the land I swore to their ancestors to give them. Be strong and very courageous. Be careful to obey all the law my servant Moses gave you; do not turn from it to the right or to the left, that you may be successful wherever you go. Keep this Book of the Law always on your lips; meditate on it day and night, so that you may be careful to do everything written in it. Then you will be prosperous and successful. Have I not commanded you? Be strong and courageous. Do not be afraid; do not be discouraged, for the Lord your God will be with you wherever you go."

My willingness to go from being a friend straight to marriage is often questioned. I'm standing on God's word. Placing my trust in the gift giver (God) and not in the gift (my best friend). From this day forward the only earthly man that gets to experience ALL of this woman will be my husband. I avoided meeting my best friend's representative, the person one pretends to be, because we are friends first. Friends with no motives. This brought out the genuine side of us. Neither of us were trying to impress the other. And he accepts me just the way that I am. It's all in God's timing. I will allow pursuit, and go on dates with him, when God allows. As of right now, I'm being OBEDIENT to God saying I have to leave him behind. At first clueless as to what that meant, or even looked like. We get to see each other on Sundays at church, Tuesdays during the youth choir rehearsal, and some Wednesdays after bible study. Every once in a while God allows us to be at the same event such as the Pastor's Conference that just took place at the Galt House. We take full advantage of moments like this that God allows and focus on enjoying one another's company. We never know when the next opportunity will be. This time apart I've been able to see God is working on us individually and it's truly growing our love for each other to be even stronger.

God showed me the importance of an OBEDIENT wife. I found it odd that everyone else that God said I needed to leave behind, He told me directly. When it came to my best friend, God spoke to my best friend first and my best friend had to tell me. Originally, I questioned if that's what God said, because of that challenging thing I do. It was confirmed several times with God's word in *1 Samuel 9:27*. I wondered, why is this Lord? Why did you give me warning and direction about the others, and not him? God answered saying that, He gives the order to the husband *(Adam, Genesis 2:16)* and it's a wife's position *(Eve, Genesis 3:2 shows that she knew the commandment)* to remind the husband what God spoke to him. This blew my mind! It wasn't until I was OBEDIENT to the voice of God that my best friend fell in line. This helped me to see that women really have more power than we think. If a wife submits to what God is telling her husband, God can work, transform, become and do so much more in his life. Like Adam, *Genesis 3:6,* men just eat the apple that is given to them. God showed me that a wife can hold her husband up, when she doesn't play her position and refuses to obey the order given. When wives think they have to be girlfriends too, husbands are being held up. God is saying, No, be his wife and submit yourself! A girlfriend has a choice. A girlfriend submits to neither God or a husband. You give up your right of it being a choice when you say "Yes" to God and "I do" to your husband.

I knew I had to go as much as we wanted to hold on to each other. I wouldn't have had the time to dedicate to writing this book and carry out the assignment God has given me. I would have naturally done what I've always done and play wife to another boyfriend and God didn't want that for me. Filling my time up with my best friend and his kid's needs. Leave him behind because more than likely we would have eventually done things our own way and burned with passion. Leave because God has been doing a work in me, him, and his children as well. Leave him behind simply because God said so.

Being OBEDIENT shows my best friend that I'm already a wife that knows how to submit, because my life is first submitted to God. This shows me that I could submit to him as my husband, because he is in tune with the voice of God. If it's the Lord's will that I marry my best friend, I pray that he will work the same passion as Jacob worked for Rachel *(Genesis 29)*, and I pray I help him to fulfill his purpose like Leah.

That he favors me how Elkanah favored Hannah *(1 Samuel 1)* and I birth with him something we can give back to God. That we create a love store like *Song of Solomon*. Like Joseph, he will trust whatever spiritual gift God has conceived in me *(Matthew 1)*. That he cries out to God in prayer on my behalf like Moses did for Miriam *(Numbers 12)*. He is as obedient as Abraham *(Genesis 12)*, and be a man like David, after God's own heart *(1 Samuel 13)*. Like Boaz, he be willing to bare all that comes with me *(Ruth 4)*. That he loves me as Christ loves me *(John 15)*.

    I don't believe God was just talking about praying, when he said he wanted my best friend and I to "do it." We've been told that we're too deep and a lot of people don't understand our way of doing things. What they don't understand is that this isn't our way, it's God's way. We're wise enough to know that in the past we have messed this thing up so many times, that we'd much rather be OBEDIENT and do it God's way, under His instructions. Even if it doesn't always make sense to us. Every chance my best friend gets he lets me know he's coming for me! Until the day comes that a man finds this good thing, this wife, I will gladly live in my 1Corinthian 7, unmarried state. Better! Allowing pursuit, and dates, when God allows. No longer expecting God to bless a worldly ritual, into becoming a holy matrimony. Becoming one with the Lord, enjoying the state I'm in. Experiencing the goodness of the Lord. I will no longer be a girlfriend to anyone else and God intended so much more.

Marriage isn't guaranteed for everyone, but I won't sell myself short just to have someone. I'll remain submitting my life unto the Lord.

I'm no one's girlfriend & OBEDIENCE got me here

Who are you submitted to?
> My greatest failures help produce my greatest product!
> *I'm no one's girlfriend & OBEDIENCE got me here.*

> "So then, just as you received Christ Jesus as Lord, continue to live your lives in him, rooted and built up in him, strengthened in the faith as you were taught, and overflowing with thankfulness."

Colossians 2:6

More Inspiring Worship Songs that ministered to me during thus process

You are my Strength – William Murphy (this song is how I start everyday)
You alone are God- Marvin Sapp (My favorite Gospel song)
Press in your presence, Give me you, never be the Same- Shana Wilson-
I Trust You – James Fortune and Fiya
Encourage Yourself – Donald Lawrence
Amazing – Ricky Dillard
Lord you are Good – Todd Garbeth
Son of Man-, You can change- Tye Tribbett
So Amazing- Hezekiah Walker
At your feet – Valencia Lacey
We give you glory – James Fortune
There is a King in You- Donald Lawrence
God Cares for you- Vashawn Mitchell
Worth Fighting for – Brian Courtney Wilson
Great Shepherd , You are welcome- Psalmist Raine
Broken Vessels- Hillsong
The Anthem- The Planet Shakers
Let Your Power Fall- James Fortune
You Waited- Travis Greene
Best Days- Tamela Mann
Yesterday- Mary Mary
War-Charles Jenkins- Todd Dulaney
Victory Belongs to Jesus
Greater Than Album– Tye Tribbett
How Can it be Album- Lauren Daigle
Withholding Nothing Album- William McDowell
The Hill Album -Travis Greene
The Sound Album -William Murphy
God Chaser Album- William Murphy
Demonstrate Album- William Murphy
Grace Album-Tasha Cobb
One Place Album- Tasha Cobb
Heart Passion Pursuit Album, - Tasha Cobb
Losing my Religion -Kirk Franklin
The Truth- Casey J
Life Music: Stage two – Johnathon McReynolds

The Word Say's

Find you a secret place!

"And when you pray, do not be like the hypocrites, for they love to pray standing in the synagogues and on the street corners to be seen by others. Truly I tell you, they have received their reward in full. But when you pray, go into your room, close the door and pray to your Father, who is unseen. Then your Father, who sees what is done in secret, will reward you. And when you pray, do not keep on babbling like pagans, for they think they will be heard because of their many words. Do not be like them, for your Father knows what you need before you ask him. "This, then, is how you should pray:
"Our Father in heaven, hallowed be your name, your kingdom come, your will be done, on earth as it is in heaven. Give us today our daily bread. And forgive us our debts, as we also have forgiven our debtors. And lead us not into temptation, but deliver us from the evil one."
Matthew 6: 5-13

Remain Humble!

"If my people, who are called by my name, will humble themselves and pray and seek my face and turn from their wicked ways, then I will hear from heaven, and I will forgive their sin and will heal their land. Now my eyes will be open and my ears attentive to the prayers offered in this place."
2 Chronicles 7: 14-15

Die to flesh! Humility!
"For to me, to live is Christ and to die is gain"
Philippians 1:21

Repent, and turn away!

"Repent, then, and turn to God, so that your sins may be wiped out, that time of refreshing may come from the Lord, and that he may send the Messiah, who has been appointed for you- even Jesus"
Acts 3:19 -20

I've never physically given birth, but I have been in situations needing someone to tell me to "keep pushing" or, "Your almost there"
When the birthing part is over, you forget about the pain you had to endure!

"I consider that our present sufferings are not worth comparing with the glory that will be revealed in us.
We know that the whole creation has been groaning as in the pains of childbirth right up to the present time." *Romans 8: 18 & 22*

God will restore!
"And the God of all grace, who called you to his eternal glory in Christ, after you have suffered a little while, will himself restore you and make you strong, firm and steadfast."
1Peter 5:10

"Above all else, guard your heart, for everything you do flows from it."
Proverbs 4:23

"Charm is deceptive, and beauty is fleeting; but a woman who fears the Lord is to be praised. Honor her for all that her hands have done, and let her works bring her praise at the city gate." *Proverbs 31:30-31*

Acknowledgements

      I would like to thank God, my Father in Heaven, for giving me the idea, vision, and desire to want to put my life story in a book. Thank you for choosing me! Thank you for my life! Being able to put a portion of my walk with you in book form, makes every trial faced and every obstacle I overcame worth it. I thank you for times of suffering; it worked for my good. Thank you for restoring my life! I thank you Father for not giving up on me when I gave up on myself. Thank you for trusting me and sharing your heart with me. Father I admire your love for me; it's unconditional! My heart is grateful for the blessing of Abraham over my life! Grateful for the generational curses broken from my life! Thank you for direction, guidance, and each time you brought me to a place of surrender. Your consistency makes it easier to follow you, even when I lack understanding. Thank you the great I Am! Thank you for the invite into partnership with your son, Jesus Christ. I'm trusting you for everything you have shown me regarding this book, my future, and my ministry. I remain confident, that I will see the goodness of you Lord. I give ALL glory back to you for what has happen and what will happen in my life. I love you with my whole heart.

      Pastor Vincent E. James Sr. Thank You! Thank you for your leadership, your passion for the will of God to be prevailed, and your motivation and investment in me. Thank you for being more than a spiritual father, but an earthly father as well. Thank you for walking in your gift not only serving as Pastor, but as Prophet and teacher. Thank you for sitting at the feet of Jesus so you can hear clearly from Him, and speak not your own words, but a fresh word from the Lord. You have guided and instructed me anytime I called you. I'm so grateful that you trusted me to serve as Worship Leader, Youth Choir Director, and in so many other capacities under your authority as my Pastor. I'm blessed to be able to sow into fertile ground. The Lord promised the same favor that rest on your life rest on my life. I pray God continue to bless you and your family with abundance.

      To my mother and father, Michael and Lena Neely, thank you for your constant love. prayers and support. The independent woman you raised tries not to call and ask for much; anytime I do, you always come through. Allowing me to cleave when necessary. Thank you for wanting me to always have the best, and always giving your very best!

Thank you to my entire family. To my siblings, Antonio Perks, Michael Neely Jr., and Charles Neely, thank you for allowing me to be the spoiled girl that I am!! Please remember y'all are not my daddy, but my brothers! Aunties and Uncles thank you for being second parents to me. Always making yourselves available and being supportive of my dreams as if I were your own child. Aunts: Janice Stone, Barbara Perks, Terri Rice, Carmelita Weakley and Uncles: Darron Stone Sr. and Eugene Rice. To my cousins, I love y'all! All the best memories include you all. Renesha Stone, Darron Stone Jr., Maurice Stone Sr., Earlisha Stone, Antwan Perks, Jessica Perks, Natalya Perks, Kentera Obin, Jeff Pleasant (uncle Jeff lol), and Seth Petway. To the daycare of kids: Andrea, Jada, Dariona, Christopher, Dakara, D3, Lariyah, TJ, Leah, Jacob, Moe Moe, Mauri, Dylan, Samuel, and the one Auntie (Earl) is now carrying; Aunt Nee is still and will always be the coolest auntie/ godmother you can have! Don't forget it. I love each of you equally.

To Mr. Channing L. Banks. Thank you! Thank you for being my brother in Christ, and my best friend. You have helped set the standard so high as to how I allow people to treat me. Thank you for not growing angry because I didn't want to be your girlfriend. Thank you for teaching me, knowing me, and accepting me. Thank you for loving me, I love you.

To all my girls, my sisters: Charlotte Hazelwood to many the stories in these pages are news to them. You however, was there during the healing of it all. Every tear shed I love you girl! Lisa Stringer, Sekeithia Gardner, Tajuana Bradshaw, LaQueisha Bonds, Verona Hardimon, and Lisa Lee Williams, thank you for the pruning experience. Lakena Smalley, Nicohle Boller, Lakeshea Cameron, Shonda Martin, Brittney Harrison, Brittney Reed, Fhonia Ellis, Erica Bledsaw, Rachel Lewis, Tramiane Anthony, Gee Dean, and Sheverra Williams thank you for your listening ears and shoulders to cry on.

To the Ladies of J'adore Unlimited! Kierra Taylor and DeQwandra Van Irvin thank you for helping to birth something new. I look forward to our future together.

To my clients, it's far too many to name, but please know how much I appreciate you. Thank you for allowing me to provide you with a service. Thank you for trusting me with your secrets; for sharing your special moments in life with me. Thank you for following me from salon to salon and trusting the God given talent that I have. Thank you for giving and receiving; giving hope and encouragement and being able to receive it as well. Thank you for challenging me to be better. I spend more time with you all than anywhere else. Thank you for making that time meaningful. Thank you for your support, patience, comfort, and your love! You all are more than clients to me, God has strategically placed each of you in my life/chair, for a reason, and I'm grateful that He trust me with you, and that you trust me as well.

To Elim Baptist Church, y'all are the BOMB!! Each opportunity that I get to minister before you, makes me want to be and do better. You keep me in my word and at the feet of Jesus. I don't want to just present you with anything, so I'm constantly going to the throne. Elim has allowed me to be a student and a teacher. Thank you for sharpening me and thank you for letting me practice ministry on you first. I grew up spiritually, physically, and mentally at this place. Elim is family! We are Elim 100%!

To all my friends and family, my Oak Grove Missionary Baptist Church family, any stylist I've had the honor of working next to, to any church that has allowed me to come and minister in song, associates, social media friends, and anyone that may purchase this book, Thank You! To the youth that I get to serve and be an example for, Thank You! Knowing that you are watching me, makes me want to strive to get it right. Ms. Janee' Love's yall!

To Erica Bledsaw of Erica Denise Ent. Thank You! I couldn't have done this without you. Only God knew what he was doing that night! I pray much success in all areas of your life; that the windows of Heaven be open for you! That you never experience lack again! I pray the Lord create and provide resources so that all your dreams come true. Thank You! Thank You! Thank You!

Thank you to everyone that I ever played a girlfriend to. You helped me to build my ark.

Made in the USA
Columbia, SC
26 April 2018